Controlling
Diabetes
the Easy Way

Controlling
Diabetes
the Easy Way

Originally published as *Diabetes: Controlling
It the Easy Way* by Random House, Inc., in 1981

STANLEY
MIRSKY, M. D.
and
JOAN RATTNER
HEILMAN

RANDOM HOUSE 🏠 NEW YORK

Grateful acknowledgment is made to The New American Library for permission to reprint "19 Popular Food Items," adapted from *Calories and Carbohydrates*, 4th Edition, by Barbara Kraus. Copyright © 1971, 1973, 1975 by Barbara Kraus. Copyright © 1979, 1981 by The New American Library, Inc. Reprinted by arrangement with The New American Library, Inc., New York, N.Y.

Library of Congress Cataloging in Publication Data

Mirsky, Stanley, 1929–
    Controlling diabetes the easy way.

    Rev. and updated ed. of: Diabetes—controlling it
the easy way. 1982, c1981.
    Includes index.
    1. Diabetes—Diet therapy. 2. Low-carbohydrate
diet. I. Heilman, Joan Rattner. II. Mirsky,
Stanley, 1929–   . Diabetes—Controlling it the
easy way. 1982, c1981. III. Title.
    RC662.M57   1985   616.4'620654   84–18308
    ISBN 0–394–72674–X

Manufactured in the United States of America
B987654

To Susan, Jennifer and Jonathan

*Also to the memory of my mentor,
Dr. Elliott P. Joslin, 1869–1962.*

Gladly would he learn, and gladly teach.

Contents

Introduction

Even though diabetes is one of the most common chronic diseases, it has never been easy for the millions of diabetics to find rational answers to their questions about it. For many people, their condition seems to present a situation so complicated that they are overwhelmed and confused. They feel dominated by the diagnosis and the life style it often imposes.

The purpose of this book is to counter the misconceptions and fears about diabetes, to give straightforward, easy-to-understand explanations of what this age-old disease actually is, where it comes from, how to cope with it and how to minimize its effect on your life.

It's impossible to know too much about your diabetes. The more you know, the more control you will have over your own destiny. For this is a disease that requires you to be your own doctor much of the time.

In this book you will find clear information about every aspect of diabetes, with special emphasis on diet—your major weapon. I have been a specialist in diabetes for many years, and recommend for what to many is the simplest, easiest, most effective diet plan that has ever been proposed for controlling blood sugar. It is so easy, in fact, that you have only to remember just one rule and know how to count to fifty.

Included also is a special chapter for hypoglycemics—people who suffer from low blood sugar. Though hypoglycemics are not diabetics, they, too, have a problem maintaining a normal blood-sugar level, and will therefore also benefit from the same dietary plan.

—Stanley Mirsky, M.D., New York, N.Y. May, 1981

Controlling Diabetes the Easy Way

ONE

What It Means to Be a Diabetic

Noвору is delighted to be diagnosed as a diabetic. After all, diabetes is a chronic disease with serious consequences and complications if it isn't kept under control. You must watch what you eat, get regular exercise and maybe take pills or insulin injections. It is a condition that you will have for the rest of your days. So far, there is no cure.

But diabetes is the one major disorder whose effects on your life style depend to a remarkable degree on how much you know, and how much effort and time you are willing to spend paying attention to it. You can minimize the impact it has on your daily life as well as your future health simply by learning all about it and then living with a few rules that actually would make everyone in the world healthier if they, too, abided by them. At best, you may lose all evidence of diabetes. At least, you may be able to reduce the amount of medication you require—all as the result of eating sensibly. The easy-to-follow diet presented here may change your life.

About 10 million Americans are diabetic (though many of them don't know it), and every year the incidence increases about 6 percent. A newborn baby who lives to be seventy now has a 1-in-5 chance of becoming diabetic. A federal commission reported in 1975 that the incidence of diabetes had increased by over 50 percent from 1965 to 1973, and that the disease and its complications are responsible for more than 300,000 deaths a year. This makes it the third largest killer after heart disease and cancer.

A recent study estimates the cost of diabetes to be about $15 billion a year—$5.7 billion in direct costs, including hospitalization and treatment, and over $10 billion in lost productivity.

To give you all the bad news at once, diabetics are much more likely to become blind, lose a foot or a leg, have kidney failure, hardening of the arteries and other difficulties.

Now for the good news. Tremendous progress has been made in only the last few years in the prevention and treatment of the disease. It is very likely that a cure will be discovered soon. Most diabetics who not long ago would have died at an early age or would have existed with such dire complications that life would have been hardly worth living, can now lead almost normal lives and can look forward to a respectable, reasonably healthy old age.

Here are some of the statistical facts about diabetes:

• Over 85 percent of the 6,000,000 diagnosed diabetics in the United States are "non-insulin-dependent." If they follow the correct diet, this group, formerly known as maturity-onset diabetics, may never require insulin except perhaps during periods of stress. The remaining less than 15 percent are "insulin-dependent." Formerly called juvenile-onset diabetics, this group will always need insulin and cannot get along with diet alone or with oral antidiabetic agents. These are two separate disorders, although they have many of the same problems.

• It has been estimated that about 2 million American diabetics take insulin by injection, about 1½ million take oral antidiabetic drugs and the remainder of the diagnosed diabetics are treated with diet only.

• Women are twice as likely to get diabetes as men.

• The chances of developing diabetes double with every 20 percent of excess weight and with every 10 years of increasing age.

• Blacks are 20 percent more likely than whites to have diabetes, and poor people have three times more chance of diabetes than middle- and upper-income people. Orientals and Eskimos rarely have it.

What Is Diabetes?

Diabetes mellitus is a metabolic disorder that results in persistent *hyper*glycemia—an abnormally high amount of sugar in the blood, usually over 140 mg percent before eating or over 200 mg percent two hours after a meal. (On the other hand, *hypoglycemia* means the opposite—an abnormally *low* blood-sugar level.) It is thought today that diabetes is actually several different diseases with different causes, all with the same result: the inability of the body to efficiently utilize the carbohydrates we eat as a source of fuel. Glucose, the end product of carbohydrate metabolism, is the body's primary fuel. It is used immediately for energy, or it is stored in the liver in the form of glycogen to be called upon at a later time.

When the body is unable to metabolize carbohydrates, which are derived mainly from sugars and starches, the blood becomes overloaded with glucose. The kidneys are unable to handle the excess and in most cases it is "spilled" into the urine.

What's Gone Wrong?

If you have diabetes, something has gone awry in the elaborate system of metabolic checks and balances the normal body uses to maintain a safe blood-sugar level. Sometimes the pancreas, a large gland located on the left side under the ribs, completely abdicates its job of turning out insulin, the hormone that helps the cells to use glucose as their fuel. Sometimes the pancreas secretes an inadequate amount of insulin, not enough to cope with the carbohydrates you eat. And sometimes the pancreas is unable to "recognize" the high blood-sugar level and so does not produce enough insulin in response to it even though the capacity is there.

In most cases, however, especially in older overweight diabetics, the pancreas continues to produce plenty of insulin, often much more than normal. But the insulin cannot perform its function of helping the cells to use glucose. The reason is a shortage of insulin receptors, areas on the cell membranes that allow insulin to permeate the cell walls. A whole cell, for example, usually has about 30,000 receptors, of which about 10 percent, or 3,000, are at work at any one time. Research has found that, in a susceptible person, overeating and a large weight gain increase the production of insulin, which then causes a reduction in the number of receptors. Plentiful insulin floats uselessly in the blood, unable to penetrate the cells, while sugar piles up but cannot be utilized.

How Does Your Body Make Insulin?

Insulin is manufactured by complicated little biochemical "factories" in the pancreas. These are the beta cells, responsible for so much of our well-being. They are located in the islets of Langerhans, one to two million tiny areas of the pancreas comprising maybe 2 percent of the entire gland.

The islets also secrete other hormones—glucagon from the alpha cells and somatostatin from the delta cells, for example—which are deposited along with insulin into the bloodstream via the tiny blood vessels that surround them. All three hormones are involved in maintaining normal blood-sugar levels.

When it is working normally, the pancreas responds to every minute fluctuation in blood sugar, releasing insulin whenever it is needed just as a thermostat turns a furnace off and on to maintain a constant temperature in your house. When the blood sugar rises after we eat, a signal goes to the pancreas, alerting it to move some insulin out.

When there is not enough glucose in the bloodstream to be used for fuel, the liver, stimulated by the glucagon from the islets' alpha cells, releases glucose from its warehouse of stored glycogen. When a sufficient amount has been secreted, somatostatin is responsible for turning off the production before it goes too high.

It takes most people about two to three hours to return to the normal fasting blood-sugar level after a high-carbohydrate meal.

How Is Insulin Used?

In the normal person, starches, sugars and proteins (58 percent of which is eventually converted into carbohydrate), are broken down by the intestines into glucose, a form of sugar. The glucose is carried throughout the body by the bloodstream, entering the cells with the help of insulin, then burned for energy by the muscles. Some of the leftovers are stored in the muscle cells or converted into fat. The rest is stockpiled in the liver in the form of glycogen, to be called upon later if the blood sugar falls too low.

If there is not enough insulin or if the insulin available cannot help the glucose permeate the cells, this sugar accumulates in the blood, often in very high concentrations. The result is diabetes.

In a nondiabetic, glucose concentration is usually below 115 milligrams per 100 milliliters of blood plasma, and even after a huge overload of sugar rarely goes above 160 to 180 mgs. In uncontrolled diabetics, it can go much higher, frequently reaching 800 or even 1,000 mgs. Though there's obviously plenty of glucose available to feed the body's hungry tissues, it cannot be used effectively and the cells can literally starve, no matter how much you eat.

At the same time, the liver is stimulated to release its stores of sugar and then to begin a process called gluconeogenesis. In a response to an emergency call for more fuel, this important organ takes the huge amounts of amino acids produced by the starving tissues and changes them into more glucose. Fats are also transported to the liver. Now ketones, the end products of the burning of fat for fuel instead of carbohydrate, also overload the kidneys and spill into the urine. When this happens, and nothing is done to remedy the situation, the body lapses into a diabetic coma—a real emergency.

Non-Insulin–Dependent Diabetes Mellitus ("Maturity-Onset")

The vast majority of diabetics are NIDDMs. If you are in this category, you continue to manufacture insulin, perhaps not enough to cover your needs, or perhaps more than enough, but it cannot be efficiently utilized. You can probably control your diabetes with diet, or diet combined with oral hypoglycemic drugs that stimulate the release of insulin or lower your blood sugar. Or you may require insulin injections to supplement your own supply. Only about 10 to 15 percent of NIDDMs take medication regularly.

Though your diabetes may have been uncovered after you developed specific symptoms such as excessive thirst and urination, more likely you were diagnosed during a routine medical checkup. Or maybe your eye doctor or dentist was the first to suspect it. Most cases of NDDM occur gradually, and so don't present obvious warning signals.

Even teenagers may have this variety of diabetes (about 5 percent of NIDDMs are under twenty), but statistically it is probably likely to occur in people over forty, becoming more common by age fifty or sixty.

Most NIDDMs have inherited a tendency toward diabetes. Eighty-five percent have a diabetic parent or other close relative.

What's more, they are almost always overweight. The vast majority of maturity-onset diabetics are too heavy. Many overweight NIDDMs can lose their diabetes by losing weight. Sometimes a loss of even a few pounds is sufficient to accomplish this miracle; as a result, you may produce enough of your own insulin to keep your blood sugar normal or increase the number of cell receptor sites so that the insulin you produce can be utilized properly.

The number of receptors and the ability of the insulin to bind to them are also increased by exercise. In controlled studies, it has been discovered that regular, vigorous exercise can lower or even eliminate the need for pills or injections.

All maturity-onset diabetes is not the result of overweight in a predisposed person. Sometimes it's simply the result of an inefficient pancreas. The beta cells become unable to sense the sugar molecules and respond accurately to their presence; or they simply cannot produce enough insulin. In these cases, losing weight won't help but eating correctly and exercising enough will, perhaps supplemented by oral agents or insulin.

Insulin-Dependent Diabetes Mellitus ("Juvenile-Onset")

"Juvenile" diabetes is quite another story and may even be another disease with similar outcome. There are comparatively few IDDMs—less than 15 percent of the total number of diabetics.

IDDM can strike at any age and about 15 to 20 percent of IDDMs are adults when they are diagnosed. But it happens for most people before they are twenty, and most commonly around the ages of eight, twelve and puberty, when dramatic growth spurts take place. For every 100,000 people in the country, there are 50 diagnosed diabetics under the age of five; there are 150 under the age ten; 270 below fifteen; and 325 per 100,000 population by the age of eighteen.

If you are an IDDM, you have a marked insufficiency in the number of beta cells your pancreas possesses and you produce little or no insulin of your own. That means you must take insulin injections to compensate. Except in extremely rare cases, the oral drugs, designed to stimulate production in a pancreas that has the capability to make its own insulin, won't work for you.

Unlike NIDDM, IDDM generally shows up very abruptly and dramatically, with unmistakable symptoms—excessive urination and thirst, dramatic weight loss, weakness, irritability. If these symptoms go untreated, they rapidly progress into acidosis and finally coma in only a few days or weeks.

As an IDDM, you probably do not have diabetic parents, though there is a genetic factor here too, as studies with identical twins have shown. Far from overweight, you are probably very thin and perhaps wan. There is no way for you to lose your symptoms by losing weight and eating sanely. But supplementary insulin, aided by good diet and plenty of exercise, will keep your blood sugar relatively normal.

The Causes of Diabetes

Heredity plays a very important role for the NIDDM. We know there must be a genetic predisposition, perhaps resulting in early aging of the pancreatic cells. When some kind of stress—overweight or pregnancy, for example—is added to the genetic tendency, diabetes is the result.

The genetically isolated Pima Indians who live in a remote river valley in the Arizona desert tend to be both obese and diabetic. Half of the Pimas over thirty-five have diabetes, 15 times the incidence among the general population in the United States, the highest rate ever recorded. The sumo wrestlers of Japan, too, are programmed to gain tremendous amounts of weight. They are adored by the sportsmen of Japan, but develop diabetes and heart disease early in their lives. They blaze like meteors across the sky, but the trip is short.

Both groups are good examples of the inherited tendencies toward this disease combined with obesity. If you have a family history of NIDDM, it would be extremely wise not to get fat.

For the IDDM, the "juvenile" diabetic, the theory today is that the disease is triggered by a virus that infects the beta cells of a susceptible person who has inherited a defective gene from both parents. The infection then sets off an autoimmune reaction. This means that antibodies are produced in response to the infection, circulate in the bloodstream, react to pancreatic beta cells as if these cells were foreign invaders and knock them permanently out of commission. The suspected triggering viruses include Coxsackie B_4, mumps and German measles.

Many genetic markers for diabetes have been identified only recently. If a child has genetic material DR3 or DR4 on his sixth chromosome, inherited from *both* parents, he has 2½ times more chance of becoming diabetic after a viral infection. Eighty-five to 90 percent of all type I diabetics have DR3 and/or DR4. A second indicator is the presence of cytoplasmic pancreatic-islet-cell antibodies, found in 80 to 90 percent of children destined to become diabetics. But if, like the Eskimos, a child has B7 on the sixth chromosome, his chances of diabetes are decreased. And if he has DR2, it is extremely doubtful he will get diabetes. Though people with DR2 make up a quarter of the population, only a few cases of diabetes have ever been reported among them.

Occasionally, diabetes is the result of another physical condition: pancreatitis, tumors, adrenal imbalance, injury to or removal of the pancreas or damage caused by several drugs. Some investigators have reported that birth control pills may trigger the onset of diabetes in predisposed women.

Who Gets Diabetes?

Diabetes gives geneticists headaches because it is almost impossible to predict, even in the presence of defective genes, who will eventually become diabetic. It was once thought that all the children of two diabetic parents would eventually become diabetic. Today it is thought that 60 percent is a more accurate figure.

With one diabetic parent, sibling or child, there is a 3

percent chance of diabetes by the age of forty to fifty-nine, a 10 percent chance after sixty.

The identical twin of a person who becomes diabetic before forty has a 30 percent likelihood of developing the disease. If the disease has its onset after forty, the chance an identical twin will have it increases to 75 percent, but if the disease does not occur within three years, the identical twin's chances drop substantially. Fraternal twins, by the way, have about the same incidence as other family members—about 10 percent.

Everything's Under Control

Once you know you are diabetic, you've got a new goal in life: to keep your blood sugar as close to normal as you possibly can. That means, ideally, between 70 mgs percent fasting and 150 mgs after a meal. That's not easy, especially in times of stress when every diabetic's blood sugar runs rampant, but you can stay within that range most of the time if you remember your future depends on it.

For many years, it was thought that this tight control was not too important as long as you felt well and functioned normally. Today we know differently. Uncontrolled diabetes—consistently high blood sugars—can eventually affect every system of the body, resulting in many exotic varieties of diabetic complications. We now know it is vital to maintain good control to avoid or minimize these effects. A recently published 30-year study of 4,400 diabetics revealed that those people who had held their blood-sugar levels to below 300 mgs had three times less risk of complications after fifteen years of the disease than those with higher levels. Those with a level below 250 mgs had 5 to 20 times less risk. And those who kept their blood sugar below 120 on diet alone had almost no risk of complications at all.

In a study of the Pimas, it was found that complications occurred in the group with fasting sugars above 140 and above 200 two hours after eating. The higher the sugar, the more likely the complications.

Of course, life is not fair, as President John F. Kennedy once said. Some people who pay no attention to their control never develop complications in spite of their lack of vigilance, while others who exercise great care do get them in later years. But, in general, it is true that greater control means a better, healthier, longer life.

Nobody's perfect, and you won't be either. You will not always follow your diet plan, you will succumb to temptation now and then, you'll forget to test your urine sometimes, you will let your control get out of hand. But remember, if this becomes your pattern and not just an occasional slip-up, you will undoubtedly pay the piper later. All the health problems associated with diabetes are hastened and exacerbated by poor control.

Who's In Charge Around Here?

You are. Your doctor will diagnose and prescribe and direct your treatment, but you are the only one who can live your own life. You're the one who puts the food into your mouth, decides how much exercise to get, makes the urine tests every day, handles the crises of hypoglycemia and high blood sugar. You can get direction and advice from your doctor and this book, but you are in charge of yourself.

This does not mean you are out there all on your own. It is very important that you see your doctor frequently, whether or not you take insulin. The doctor monitors your blood-sugar control in order to prevent complications in the future, picks up early changes, works with you on problems concerning diet, exercise, life style, or whatever, and advises you on handling illnesses.

If you are a diabetic who is regulated by diet alone, see your doctor *at least* every three months. Don't go whenever you feel like it, or when trouble brews. Go regularly on a scheduled basis.

If you take oral agents or insulin, make an appointment even more often, depending on your condition. Once a month is right for most people. Don't skip or postpone an appointment if you can possibly avoid it.

To find a doctor who can give you good care, call your local chapter of the American Diabetes Association or of the Juvenile Diabetes Foundation. You will be given the names of several doctors in your area who are the most knowledgeable about diabetes. This is a specialized field, and many general physicians are not qualified to handle your problems. Your future will be much brighter if you find a doctor who is.

Living with diabetes means a constant balancing act between the food you eat and the insulin you produce yourself or take by injection, along with the exercise you get. Insulin provides the mechanism for burning the food for energy to run your complex body. Exercise lowers your blood-sugar level. If you eat more food, you will need more insulin and exercise. If you eat less food, you will require less insulin and exercise. That's simple. What's hard is always having to think about this balancing act especially at times when, through no fault of your own, this balance is thrown out of kilter.

For many people, one of the most trying aspects is the need to be consistent, to lead a structured life. Especially if you take insulin, you soon discover that you must eat a preordained amount of carbohydrate, that you must eat on time, take your medication on schedule, make constant urine or blood tests, check in with your doctor regularly. While everyone else, it seems, can stay up all night partying, eating pizza and drinking sodas, "pigging out" one day and fasting the next, paying no attention to medicines or doctors, you, if you are on insulin, must plug along, day after day, on three meals plus two snacks.

That can be difficult, but it will pay off. Consistency isn't such a tremendous price to pay for feeling well now and in the future. It will eventually become a life style you can live with.

TWO

Are You
a Hypoglycemic?

THE word *hypo*glycemia simply means "low blood sugar," nothing more or less. (Hyperglycemia—diabetes—is the opposite, meaning "high blood sugar.") The number of people diagnosed as "hypoglycemics" has grown to enormous porportions in the last few years. In reality a rare phenomenon (except as an insulin reaction among diabetics), hypoglycemia has been blamed for a variety of strange feelings and symptoms that seem to require a label and an explanation, has made fortunes for many doctors, nutritionists and quacks, and has been both overdiagnosed and underdiagnosed. We all know people who have been told, or have decided, they have chronic low blood sugar. Most of them could not honestly be called hypoglycemic. On the other hand, there are unsuspecting people who do have consistent low blood sugar at times during the day, who suffer from symptoms as a result, are often called neurotic, and who have not been correctly diagnosed as actually having hypoglycemia, a condition, not a disease.

A "normal" blood sugar (fasting or over three hours after a meal) is considered to be between 70 or 110 mgs percent, a level that remains fairly constant because of the interaction of intestinal absorption, the liver and the pancreas.

But many people have blood sugars that drop much lower, perhaps to 40 to 50 mgs percent, and cannot be called hypoglycemic. So, how low is too low? And when does a specific number spell out hypoglycemia?

These are not easy questions to answer, but in general, a blood sugar below 50 mgs percent *that coincides with other symptoms* means you are hypoglycemic. Some people have no symptoms when their sugar is low; others may have the symptoms of hypoglycemia when their blood sugar is quite normal. No diagnosis of hypoglycemia can be made unless low blood sugar and specific symptoms *occur simultaneously.*

The Symptoms

Hypoglycemia is not dangerous, but it can make your life miserable. The symptoms may (and may not) include general weakness, fatigue, inability to concentrate, listlessness, butterfly sensations in the stomach, subnormal temperature. Also, rapid heart rate, shakiness and palpitations, sweating, and apprehension. As someone has described it, it's as if you have almost just been hit by a train.

Some hypoglycemics experience headaches, irritability, double vision, nausea, tingling, drowsiness, slurred speech and an irresistible urge to yawn. These are all associated with a low supply of glucose to the brain, which needs sugar to function. Very low drops in blood sugar can produce balance and hearing problems. Unsuccessful pregnancies have also been ascribed to hypoglycemia. In Australia, a study revealed a high incidence of perinatal deaths, as well as small placentas and small babies, among mothers who had low blood sugars. Hypoglycemia can be a powerful appetite stimulant. Many hypoglycemics gain large amounts of weight as a result.

True hypoglycemia can be compared to trying to run an eight-cylinder car on two cylinders and often is the reason for depression.

The Treatment

There is only one way to treat hypoglycemia, and that is with diet. Except in a very occasional case with an organic origin, no other treatments or medications are of any value, including injections, megavitamins and hair analysis (which will only reveal what kind of shampoo you are using).

Usually proposed for this condition is a low-carbohydrate, multiple-meals-a-day diet with an inordinate amount of fats and proteins, and insufficient carbohydrate for body fuel. It is not only difficult for most people to follow but, over the years, it can load up the arteries with fatty plaque.

The diet that works best for hypoglycemics is the same diet we recommend for diabetics. Read Chapter 4 and you will see how easy it is to live with this sensible, rational food plan that simply limits refined sugars and offers the same proportion of other carbohydrates typically eaten by Americans. With it, you will avoid the unsettling periods of reactive low blood sugar and its symptoms.

An Explanation of This Phenomenon

Hypoglycemia is often the result of too much insulin produced by the pancreas in response to an overload of sugar into the bloodstream. It may be an overreaction of the body's blood-sugar regulating system. It tends to occur in families of diabetics, but that fact does not mean all hypoglycemics will turn into diabetics one day. The current estimate is that about 50 percent of *true* hypoglycemics will one day be diabetic.

There are organic and nonorganic causes of the condition. The organic causes include tumors in the pancreas which then has no stop-and-go mechanism, allowing the beta cells to secrete insulin without regard for incoming sugar, and cirrhosis of the liver that results in little glycogen storage and glucose delivery when sugar levels fall as a result of not eating. Sometimes the adrenal glands are damaged and do not perform their vital function of converting protein into glucose for fuel. Removal of parts of the stomach because of ulcers may result in the "dumping syndrome." Without the normal sphincter tone at the lower end of the stomach, glucose is released too precipitously into the small intestine. So much glucose enters at once that insulin production cannot keep up and blood sugar rises. This triggers more insulin production, resulting in low blood sugar.

Alcoholism, too, can cause hypoglycemia. Alcohol interferes with the conversion of glucose from protein and inhibits the release of glucose from the liver's stores of glycogen. In fact, you needn't be an alcoholic but simply overindulge in order to have a hypoglycemic episode. A recent study involved 10 patients who were given three double vodka martinis for lunch. Three of them developed not only the inability to concentrate, but hypoglycemic blood-sugar levels a few hours later.

But the usual variety of hypoglycemia is nonorganic and is often an exaggerated response of the pancreas which, stimulated by large doses of sugar entering the bloodstream, pours out too much insulin. Usually, after a sugar overload, a hypoglycemic experiences a rapid rise in blood sugar to higher-than-normal levels and then a quick drop to below normal two or three hours later. Sometimes, however, the blood sugar does not rise abnormally at first, but falls below normal later.

When the sugar drops very low, the symptoms may appear. If they do, you are hypoglycemic.

Diagnosing Hypoglycemia

The best way to diagnose low blood sugar is with a glucose tolerance test, made in the doctor's office or a laboratory where results can be measured immediately after each of the several blood specimens are drawn.

The test involves drinking a large dose of glucose solution on an empty stomach and then having blood taken every hour up to five hours later. The blood is tested for glucose content. If you have hypoglycemic symptoms at any time between the scheduled testing hours, you must also be tested at that very moment. See Chapter 3 for more details.

Important: a glucose tolerance test will not give valid results if your pancreas is unprepared for it. For three or four days before the test, you *must* consume a normal amount of carbohydrate—at least 100 to 150 grams a day —so that your pancreas is not startled by the large load of sugar you will be given at one time. An unprepared pancreas can trigger a classic hypoglycemic reaction even among normal people.

Another way to test for hypoglycemia is to draw blood for testing at the moment you experience symptoms after eating normal balanced meals. If your sugar is abnormally low at these times, then you are hypoglycemic.

Living with Hypoglycemia

Let's make ourselves perfectly clear: there is no treatment for hypoglycemia except *diet*. This does not mean avoiding carbohydrates and eating mostly proteins and fats which may eventually clog your arteries. Rather, you should eat a balanced diet that consists of at least 50 to 60 percent carbohydrate. It is exactly the same food plan as a diabetic should follow.

Like diabetics, you should avoid sweets and too much quickly absorbed natural sugar that can overload the pancreas and stimulate it to pour out an excessive amount of insulin. You will probably do well on three meals a day, but if you feel better with snacks between meals there's no reason you can't have them.

The diet, described in detail in Chapter 4, will provide your body with the fuel it requires but won't overstimulate your pancreas and cause a hypoglycemic episode.

Helpful Hints

• It is wise to eat whenever you drink alcohol and to drink only moderately. Alcohol inhibits the release of glucose from the liver when it is needed by the body.

• If you are going to exercise strenuously, have a snack first. Exercise quickly depletes the blood sugar you have on board. If your vigorous activity extends over a long period of time, eat or drink some carbohydrate every hour or so.

• Coffee, tea, cocoa, chocolate, all in a chemical family called xanthines, seem to trigger hypoglycemic episodes for some people. The xanthines inhibit one of the enzymes whose function it is to tell the beta cells of the pancreas to stop producing excess insulin. So be sure to avoid these if this is true for you.

NOTE: In the remainder of this book, little else will be directed specifically to you, the hypoglycemic, though much of the information applies to you, especially in the chapters on exercise and diet. Eat properly, and your troubles will be over—it's as simple as that!

THREE

Making the Diagnosis for Diabetes

To diagnose diabetes, your doctor must confirm through tests that you have inappropriately high blood sugar—sugar that rises to abnormal heights and stays there too long. In a nondiabetic, blood sugar rises and falls throughout the day, but never goes very high or very low because the pancreas secretes sufficient and efficient insulin.

How Is Diabetes Discovered?

Many people are diagnosed as diabetics when urine or blood tests are made during routine examinations. Their symptoms are so minor that they don't even notice them. In fact, they may have had diabetes for years without knowing it. Other diabetics are discovered by their dentists who find unexplained periodontal problems, their podiatrists who spot suspicious foot sores, ophthalmologists who notice vision changes, other doctors who are looking for the underlying reasons for recurring vaginal or urinary infections, male sexual problems, menstrual irregularity, itching (especially in the genital or anal areas), tingling, numbness, or fatigue.

The Overt Symptoms

When diabetes occurs more suddenly or severely, the symptoms may be more sudden and severe too. These include the three "polys": polyuria, polydipsia and polyphagia.

Polyuria is excessive urination (when it occurs at night, it is known as excessive nocturia). When the carbohydrate you eat is not utilized, it is dumped into the urine to be excreted from the body. Urine is produced in vast amounts, the bladder fills quickly, and much of an uncontrolled diabetic's time is spent in the bathroom.

The huge loss of water from the body tissues causes dehydration. Diabetics develop *polydipsia*, a tremendous thirst that can never be satisfied.

Polyphagia, excessive hunger, is the least common of the three major symptoms. It represents the body's frantic attempt to get the fuel it requires. Even though large amounts of food may be consumed, there will be rapid weight loss. One patient, a marine sergeant, was diagnosed after he continued to lose weight even though he ate one or two pounds of meat and drank two quarts of milk and juice with every meal.

Other symptoms of diabetes include weakness, heaviness of the legs so that climbing stairs or hills becomes extremely difficult, subnormal temperature, slow healing, dizziness, acidosis and, of course, diabetic coma.

Because uncontrolled diabetes is associated with an increased incidence of heart disease, blindness, miscarriage and spontaneous abortion, these conditions may also raise the question of the possibility of diabetes in your doctor's mind.

Just a Matter of Routine

To discover hyperglycemia with a routine urine test is a matter of chance if you are not severely diabetic. The urine must be checked at just the right moment. Glucose is carried in the bloodstream and travels through the kidneys. Below a blood-sugar level of about 156 mg percent, most people will not lose sugar in the urine and it will not be discovered during the test. Instead, it will be returned to the body through the renal veins. If you have a large meal but not enough insulin, or if it is not used effectively, some sugar will turn up in the urine. But this won't happen until an hour or so after the meal, when the food has had time to be turned into glucose and has made its way to the bladder from the kidneys via the bloodstream.

Even with excess blood sugar, a test taken an hour after a meal may be so diluted with urine accumulated *before* the meal that the sugar won't show up in concentrated amounts. Two to three hours after the meal, however, the urine will reflect the higher blood sugars.

The speed of the blood flow to the kidneys also influences how much sugar appears in the urine. Sometimes, especially with diseases like heart failure, this rate drops, and, even though the sugar is high, even far above 156 mgs, very little escapes into the urine. The doctor making the diagnostic tests should take this high renal threshold into account.

In pregnancy, the reverse happens and there is an increased rate of blood flow to the kidneys. Now more sugar appears in the urine at *lower* levels. That means all pregnant women with sugar in the urine are not necessarily diabetic, though they should definitely be tested for the possibility.

The Glucose Tolerance Test

A much better diagnostic method than routine urine tests is the glucose tolerance test, which should be used any time there is any suspicion of diabetes. It is time-consuming and a little complicated, but essential. If, however, your fasting blood sugar is over 140 mgs percent, or, in two hours after eating, over 200 mgs percent on repeated blood tests, the diagnosis is already clear without a glucose tolerance test.

Before you have this test, you *must* eat at least 100 to 150 grams of carbohydrate a day for at least *three* days. This is, for most people, a normal amount. If you have been eating very little carbohydrate, the glucose tolerance test will catch your pancreas unawares and the results may not be accurate.

Diuretics and estrogen supplements may also influence a glucose tolerance test interpretation. The test is best done in the morning, sitting down and relaxed. No smoking until it is completed.

On the morning of the test, you are asked to eat no breakfast. Your first blood sample will reflect a *fasting* state —no incoming food for at least eight hours. The doctor or laboratory technician will draw a tube of blood from your arm, then give you a drink of quickly absorbed glucose. This must be swallowed within five minutes. An hour later another blood sample is drawn, followed by samples taken at two hours and three hours (and sometimes at four and five hours). The glucose content of each blood sample is carefully measured. (Note: Many doctors take a blood sample in the first half hour following the glucose intake.

The result of this provides no information useful for diagnostic purposes.)

What the Blood Tells Us

The glucose tolerance test gives readings of blood sugar for at least four different time periods—fasting, one hour, two hours, three hours. These are plotted into a curve and analyzed.

For the normal person without diabetes or hypoglycemia, blood sugar throughout the day will be between 0.070 and 0.1 grams per 100 cc of blood. In other words, whether or not the patient has recently had a meal, there is always approximately 7 to 10 parts sugar to one hundred parts of blood. This blood value of 70 to 100 mgs percent corresponds to a blood *serum* level of 115 mgs percent. The serum, the fluid left after the blood cells and blood-clotting substances are removed, is what is tested in most chemical determinations today.

In the normal person, the serum level rises an hour after eating to no more than 185 mgs percent, and at two hours drops back to no more than 145 mgs percent. At three hours, it returns to the fasting level.

But, if you are a diabetic, your numbers will be different. When your fasting level is above 140 mgs, your one-hour level above 185 mgs, two-hour level above 145, and three-hour level above 140, you have abnormally elevated glucose and you have confirmed diabetes.

Sometimes a diagnosis is made when three out of the four tests on the curve show elevated glucose, and sometimes a system of totaling the numbers is used. When the fasting, one-hour, two-hour and three-hour results are added together and produce a sum below 500, you are considered normal. From 500 to 800, you may be diabetic. With a total over 800, you are definitely diabetic.

Treatment—diet alone, or diet plus oral agents or insulin—is necessary if you have the symptoms of diabetes as well as abnormal sugars, or if you have no symptoms but have a fasting sugar over 140 and a two-hour sugar over 200.

The following chart gives examples of representative glucose tolerance tests:

TYPICAL GLUCOSE TOLERANCE TEST RESULTS

	Fasting	*1 hour*	*2 hours*	*3 hours*	*4 hours*	*5 hours*
Normal glucose	80 mgs	125 mgs	90 mgs	86 mgs	84 mgs	86 mgs
Maturity-onset Diabetic (NIDDM)	120	230	185	150	118	
Juvenile-onset Diabetic (IDDM)	250	440	300	280	250	200
Nonorganic Reactive Hypoglycemic	90	180	110	100	40	60

Impaired Glucose Tolerance

Sometimes your tests will indicate a diagnosis not of diabetes, but of "impaired glucose tolerance." This means the measurements fall somewhere between those of the normal person and the diabetic, perhaps with blood sugar becoming abnormally elevated in response to the glucose injection or drink, then returning almost to normal by the end of three hours.

If you have impaired glucose tolerance, you *don't* have diabetes. And you probably will never have it. On the other hand, you should see your doctor for a blood test once a year.

FOUR

Nobody Loves a Diet

Ask 100 people to tell you the secret of diabetes control and 99 of them will answer "insulin." They are wrong. The real secret lies not in that little white bottle, or even in small white or blue pills, but in your refrigerator and kitchen cabinets. That fact is not glamorous, mysterious or even very interesting, but it is true.

What you eat—your diet—is the single most important key to diabetic control. It is the best blood-sugar-lowering agent, the most effective and the least expensive. With diet, plus a certain amount of physical activity, you may not need insulin or oral antidiabetic agents at all. The vast majority of diabetics (and most hypoglycemics) can be controlled with diet alone. Many diabetics who now take oral agents or insulin won't need them anymore if they eat correctly. And some who are overweight will lose all their diabetic symptoms *completely* simply by taking off a few pounds.

As for those diabetics who have truly deficient pancreases and therefore require insulin injections to supply their bodies with this essential hormone, and those who can never utilize their own insulin efficiently without the help of oral agents, diet is *still* the most important ingredient of treatment. Diabetics can never achieve good control, with or without medication, unless they eat correctly.

Nobody loves a diet. Diets tell you not to eat this, and that you must eat that—no fun at all. Most people, when they are first diagnosed as diabetics, are concerned about the need to change their eating habits. After all, the majority of diabetics are overweight and they love food. They don't want to think about every bite that goes into their mouths.

But we are going to make it simple by prescribing what we believe to be the world's easiest and most effective diet. Never have diabetics (or hypoglycemics) had to think less about their food than with this plan. And yet it works.

This diet is not concerned with calories (unless, of course, you want to lose weight). It is concerned only with carbohydrates. You must eat a certain number of grams of carbohydrates (though not refined sugar) at every meal, perhaps more than you are accustomed to. That is the only rule. Aside from that, you can eat anything you like if your weight is where you want it. If you need a stricter diet, the American Diabetes Association or Joslin diets may be for you.

The diet presented here will not make you miserable, frustrated or confused. It will keep your blood sugar within the normal range that now is your chief goal. It is safe. It can be followed for a lifetime without difficulty. It is good not only for you, but for the rest of the family as well, so you won't require separate preparation of meals. As you can see, with only a little caution you can eat just like the rest of the world.

The Changing Scene in Diabetic Diets

Before the discovery of insulin in 1922, a harsh dietary regimen was the only treatment for diabetes. It usually included very little carbohydrate because once the blood sugar went up it would take off like a runaway train, precipitating a hasty demise as a result of diabetic coma. Diabetics were placed on starvation diets so low in calories that growth was retarded and they died of malnutrition if not diabetic complications; or they were given diets that included only milk and barley water boiled with bread; or rancid meats, fat and milk served up with lime water, cathartics and opium; or fat combined with alcohol and multiboiled vegetables. One nineteenth-century physician made sure his patients ate exactly what he prescribed by locking them in their rooms and opening their doors only to offer their meager food.

Once insulin was discovered, many doctors decided that patients taking injections could eat whatever they liked, which proved to be a mistake. Others still insisted that carbohydrates be kept low, perhaps to about 30 percent of the daily intake, with the major part of the calories made up of protein and fat.

Recently, however, it has been recognized that diabetics—who already have an accelecated tendency toward arteriosclerosis, heart attacks and strokes—were hastened along the road to vascular disease by the high-fat diet. The diet, in other words, was probably killing more people than it helped. In the early seventies, the American Diabetes Association recommended that diabetics eat the same proportion of carbohydrates as most other people do—50 percent or more.

But even with the liberalizing of the diet, many people continue to find it extremely difficult to stay with a plan that is rigid or complicated. We are proposing a diet that is easy to live with, simple, rational, logical. Besides, it works wherever you are. You can follow it to achieve blood-sugar levels within normal boundaries whether you eat at home, in restaurants or traveling around the world.

The World's Easiest Diabetic Diet

To follow this diet, there is just one rule: avoid all refined sugar and eat 40 to 50 grams of complex carbohydrates at every meal. (Exception: If you are engaging in strenuous exercise, you may need more.)

This carbohydrate intake will amount to 50 to 60 percent of your daily food, approximately the normal American diet. The rest of your menu will include protein, fats, water in whatever proportions you choose. If you are not trying to reduce, you may eat as much of these foods as you wish. If you are, you can control your calories up or down simply by adjusting your meat portions. Or, if you prefer, you may incorporate the food exchange lists of the American Diabetes Association to help you keep your calories counted.

Most diets designed for diabetics not only place great emphasis on cutting back carbohydrates (usually cutting them back too much), but also regulate the amount of proteins and fats you can eat at each meal. However, unless you are among a very small number of people whose control is very precarious (there are some slim people who are uncontrolled on diet or oral agents who, with a restricted calorie diet, may avoid insulin) or you are trying to lose weight, there is no need to be concerned about anything but your carbohydrate intake. You will probably consume about the same amounts of proteins and fats every day anyway, and even if you stray from your usual habits one day it won't disturb your blood sugar enough to cause problems when you are in good control. So, simply keep tabs on your carbohydrates. And relax!

The Components of Food

All foods are made up of carbohydrate, protein or fat, plus water, minerals, vitamins and fiber.

Carbohydrates (found mainly in sugar, starch, fruits and vegetables) are the natural fuel of the body and supply the energy to run all its complicated systems. If there is a shortage of carbohydrates in your diet, you will start burning fat which, in a diabetic, can lead to serious complications. Together with protein and fats, carbohydrates promote the growth and maintenance of body cells. Every gram of carbohydrate is equal to 4 calories.

Proteins are the building blocks of the body, needed for growth and repair of body tissues. Most protein foods (chiefly meat, milk, cheese, eggs, fish) contain a large proportion of fat as well. Approximately 58 percent of the protein we eat is slowly converted to carbohydrate. Each gram of protein is equal to 4 calories.

Fats provide a concentrated source of energy and add flavor to foods. They carry vitamins along with essential fatty acids, and provide cushioning for vital organs. Each gram of fat equals 9 calories.

Water is needed for all the digestive processes and is an essential part of all tissues.

Minerals and iron promote strong bones and teeth, healthy circulatory, muscular and nervous systems, blood hemoglobin, etc.

Vitamins are essential for the proper functioning of all systems of the body.

Fiber (or roughage) is not a nutrient, but important for

efficient digestion and, it is thought, helps maintain normal blood-sugar levels.

What Is a Calorie?

A calorie is the amount of energy required to raise the temperature of four gallons of water one degree Farenheit. Another way of putting it that it is the energy expended by a seated man turning a doorknob.

Though most diets are based on calorie-counting, we are not concerned here with calories—unless, of course, you want to lose weight. Then calories definitely do count because weight cannot be lost (except *temporarily* through water loss on high protein diets) without cutting some calories.

What Are Grams and Why Must We Think About Them?

It's all a numbers game. Our diet uses grams as the basic weight measurement of food. Why? Because grams are much easier to count and manipulate than ounces and pounds, and much more exact. (One pound equals 456 grams, while 1 ounce equals 30 grams. A nickel weighs 5 grams.)

It is essential for our diet to know the number of grams of carbohydrate in each food. That's because we must know how much of that food will enter the bloodstream in the form of sugar, and how quickly it will be absorbed. A diabetic or hypoglycemic can safely handle only a certain amount of sugar at one time. Too much too fast will raise a diabetic's blood sugar too high, and cause a hypoglycemic's blood sugar to rebound too low.

Every food can be analyzed into grams of carbohydrate, protein and fat. For example, a standard slice of bread weighs about one ounce or 30 grams. This slice of bread contains 15 grams of carbohydrate, 2½ grams of protein, and 12½ grams of nondigestible material and water.

A small orange weighing 100 grams contains about 10 grams of carbohydrate.

Thirty grams (1 ounce) of meat has no carbohydrate, 7 grams of protein, and 5 grams of fat. The rest is nondigestible material.

Why Concentrate on Carbohydrates?

You must know how much sugar is entering your blood-stream at any one time, because this is the main influence on your blood-sugar level. You require a certain amount, which is derived from carbohydrate, for your brain and body to function, but you cannot cope with too much.

The normal fate of 100 grams of carbohydrate eaten at one sitting is as follows: 25 grams are used by the brain and red blood cells; 60 grams are delivered to the liver to be stored as glycogen for later release or transported into the fatty-acid cycle; the remaining 15 grams are rationed out via the bloodstream to the periphery of the body to be used by the muscles at a rate of 5 grams an hour.

In the nondiabetic, this balance is always maintained by the prompt response of the pancreas to rising blood sugar. But diabetics are different. Because you produce insufficient insulin or your cells cannot absorb the glucose readily, your blood-sugar levels are not kept at the normal percentage but can rise astronomically when too much carbohydrate is eaten at one time. And they can remain high for a very long time. The excess glucose is excreted along with the urine, or it stays in the bloodstream as elevated blood sugar.

Hypoglycemics are different too. They release *too much*

insulin in response to excess sugar, clearing too much glucose from the bloodstream too quickly and so producing
very low blood sugar.

The Nitty-Gritty of Carbohydrates

Carbohydrates contain one or more chains of 3 to 7 car-
bons, 12 hydrogens, and 6 oxygens, bound together. The
smaller the number of chains, the more quickly they are
absorbed by the body. One-chain carbohydrates are mono-
saccharides, such as glucose, fructose and galactose.

Oligosaccharides are usually composed of 2 to 4 or more
chains of simple sugars, the best known being sucrose
found in cane sugar and beets, maltose found in starch and
lactose in milk.

Polysaccharides are long and complex chains of sugar
that are the readily digestible storage materials of plant
and animal cells. These are starch, dextrin and glycogen.
They are more slowly absorbed and have less immediate
effect on blood sugar.

Sorbitol and mannitol are "sugar alcohols," frequently
ingredients of "dietetic" foods. They are absorbed slowly
and the small amounts in sugarless gum or mints don't
amount to enough to affect your blood sugar unless, of
course, you eat inordinate amounts of them. You'd find that
12 pieces of sorbitol-sweetened hard candy, for example,
would affect your blood sugar. Besides, 12 pieces would
contain 150 calories and could cause diarrhea.

What You Can't Eat

Foods that contain simple carbohydrates—the monosac-
charides—must be avoided. They contain many calories
but very little nutrition. More important, they are *much*
too quickly absorbed by the bloodstream. They are too po-

tent. They are available too soon, too precipitously, to be effectively handled by diabetics or hypoglycemics. They are *dangerous* for you (except when you *need* them to raise your blood sugar in a hurry). DO NOT EAT THEM.

The simple sugars include:

Candy	Pastries and cookies
Cereals that are sugar-coated or contain sweetening	Puddings, pies and cakes
	Raisins
Condensed milk	Regular chewing gum
Dried fruits	Regular soft drinks
Honey	Sugar, any variety, any color
Jams and jellies	Sweet wine
Marmalade and preserves	Syrups
Molasses	

Other foods that diabetics and most hypoglycemics should avoid because they raise blood-sugar levels far too fast are:

Apple juice	Pineapple
Apples	Pineapple juice
Gelatin desserts (regular)	Processed yogurt with fruit or flavoring
Grape juice	
Instant breakfasts or "diet" bars	Prune juice
	Sherbet
Maple-sugar-flavored bacon or sausage	Yams and sweet potatoes

Sometimes you can be surprised by the foods that tend to raise your blood sugar too fast. For example, some people can tolerate ice cream more easily than potatoes. There has been a lot of talk recently about the "glycemic index," which means that some foods have more effect on your blood sugar than others even though they may be equivalent in carbohydrate content. You can determine what your glycemic index is for particular foods by testing your blood after you eat them, taking into account the other foods eaten in the same meal. If you find that a food sends your blood sugar rocketing, avoid it or simply eat less of it.

What You Can Eat: The Complex Carbohydrates

The complex carbohydrates, some of the oligosaccharides and the polysaccharides, are the ones that must make up your 40 ot 50 grams per meal. They are a much better source of energy than fatty foods because they have less than half the calories of fat and the same as protein, and often contain more nutrition in the form of vitamins, minerals and fiber. Besides, they can make you feel full and more satisfied.

The complex carbohydrates include grains, starches, fruits, vegetables and legumes. They are absorbed much more slowly than the simple carbohydrates and, eaten in certain amounts, won't raise your blood sugar to abnormal heights that may overwhelm your body. If you stay within the guidelines, your blood sugar should measure no more than 140 mg percent fasting and 199 mg percent two hours after a meal—just where we want it.

If you find that this is not true for you, then you must make adjustments in the food you eat. Nothing is chiseled in stone and everything can be changed to suit your special needs.

For your 40 to 50 grams of carbohydrates per meal, choose from the food lists that follow: 10-gram fruits and desserts; 15-gram starches; 3-percent vegetables; 6-percent vegetables.

Each meal must include 2 or more units from the starch list (the equivalent of 2 slices of bread). You need this slowly absorbed carbohydrate to carry you over to your next meal or snack. Fruits and juices, because they are so quickly digested and absorbed, raising your blood sugar more rapidly, *cannot be used as most or all of your total allotment.*

Keep your meals well balanced and varied, and eat the rest of your calories in proteins and fats as you like. How much of these you eat is a matter of taste and habit. Most people consume about the same amounts every day or every week. If, however, you are watching your weight or your cholesterol level, then your proteins and fats should be limited as we will discuss a little later.

Diabetics who take insulin must take care to eat the same amount of food, including the right amount of carbohydrate, every day, spaced out in the same way, because your insulin dose is based on the food you consume.

Note: You will see that we have included milk and plain yogurt in *both* the 10-gram (fruits) list and the 15-gram (starches) list. Because they are intermediate in both absorption rate and carbohydrate content, you may substitute them for foods on either list. They also contain protein and fat. Avoid the flavored and fruited yogurts. Vanilla yogurt, for example, has twice as much carbohydrate as plain. Strawberry has almost four times as much. Always check the container for carbohydrate content and figure it into your total amount for that meal.

Tomato sauce is also on two lists, the 10-gram list and the 6-percent vegetable list, because its carbohydrate content falls between the two.

Foods containing 10 grams of carbohydrate

2 medium apricots
½ medium banana
½ cup blueberries, black-
    berries or raspberries
½ small cantaloupe
9 cherries
¾ cup diet cranberry juice

¼ cup diet cranberry sauce
1 medium fresh fig
½ medium grapefruit
5 ounces grapefruit juice
15 grapes
3 medium lemons
½ small mango

⅛ large melon (honeydew)
1 medium nectarine
1 small orange
3 ounces orange juice
1 small peach
1 small pear
2 small plums
2 cups popcorn
1 cup strawberries
1 large tangerine
8 ounces (1 cup) tomato
    juice or vegetable juice
½ cup tomato sauce
1 cup watermelon balls
1 cup plain yogurt

Also:
1 scoop ice cream*
1 scoop ice milk*

½ cup evaporated milk
8 ounces (1 cup) milk†

Also:
6 animal crackers
1 "thin" slice of bread
1 slice protein bread
2 fortune cookies
3 ginger snaps
44 thin pretzel sticks
2 graham crackers
2 Lorna Doones
18 oyster crackers
5 Ritz crackers
4 saltines
3 Social Teas
3 Triscuits
2 Uneeda Biscuits
8 Wheat Thins

Foods containing 15 grams of carbohydrate

½ medium bagel
⅛ cup cooked dry beans:
    lentil, mung, pinto,
    red, garbanzo, etc.
1 slice bread (white, rye,
    pumpernickel, whole
    wheat, French, Italian)
¼ cup bread crumbs
2 bread sticks
½ small ear corn or
    ⅓ cup kernels

½ plain donut
½ English muffin
7½ medium French fries
1 slice French toast
    (made without sugar)
½ cup cooked macaroni,
    spaghetti, noodles or
    other pasta
½ matzoh
4 small matzoh balls

---

* Vanilla, chocolate, coffee or strawberry. If you eat dietetic ice cream, you may have ¼ pint, the equivalent of a 10-gram serving.
† Whole, skim, low-fat, buttermilk or powdered (¼ cup diluted with ¾ cup water).

Also:

½ cup bran cereal
  (no raisins)
½ cup cooked cereal
1 cup puffed cold cereal
  (plain)
¾ cup most other cold
  cereals
1 small corn muffin
5 thin melba toasts
1 4-inch pancake
½ large pita
½ cup mashed potatoes
1 medium white potato
½ cup cooked rice, barley,
  grits
½ hamburger roll
1 hot-dog roll
1 small plain roll

¼ cup cooked soy beans
1 piece sponge, marble or
  pound cake (same
  weight as 1 slice of
  bread) on special
  occasions
1 5-inch waffle

Also:

½ cup evaporated milk
8 ounces (1 cup) milk*
1 cup plain yogurt

1 small plain muffin or
  biscuit
2 tbsp. miller's bran
15 potato chips
2 tbsp. wheat germ (plain)
3 zwieback toasts

Note: Any item from the 10-gram list becomes 15 grams by taking one and a half portions. Be careful, however, when you consume more fruit, because it may be absorbed so quickly that it will raise your blood sugar too high. The only way to check its effect on you is to make frequent urine or blood tests.

Water-packed canned fruits may be eaten in the same amounts as fresh fruit. For example, remember that two halves of a canned pear equal 1 small pear. Don't eat more.

A Veritable Variety of Vegetables

Vegetables also contain carbohydrate, and it is important to know how much of them you can safely eat. The follow-

---

* Whole, skim, low-fat, buttermilk or powdered (¼ cup diluted with ¾ cup water).

ing list includes those that have only 3 grams of carbohydrate per 100 grams of weight and in most cases influence
your blood sugar very little. They consist mainly of water
and nondigestible fiber. Eat them raw as you like. If
cooked, limit them to about 1 cup per portion.

3-percent vegetables

Asparagus, fresh	Lettuce, romaine, chicory,
Bamboo shoots	escarole
Bean sprouts	Mushrooms
Broccoli	Parsley
Cabbage	Radishes
Cauliflower	Rhubarb (no sugar)
Celery	Sauerkraut
Cucumber	Spinach
Eggplant	Summer squash
Endive	Swiss chard
Green or wax beans	Turnip
Green pepper	Watercress
Kohlrabi	Zucchini

The 6-percent vegetables have 6 grams of carbohydrate
for every 100 grams of weight and cannot be taken ad lib
by many diabetics. These are usually restricted to ½ cup
per meal (or counted as 5 grams of your 40 to 50-gram
total). If you want to eat more, subtract appropriately
from your starch.

6-percent vegetables

Artichokes	Pumpkin
Brussels sprouts	Red peppers
Carrots	Tomatoes
Green peas	Tomato sauce
Kale	Turnips
Okra	Winter squash
Onions, leeks, chives, scallions	

The Secret of Success

The only way you can successfully stick to the 40 to 50 grams per meal of carbohydrate without constantly counting and figuring and going bananas is to remember the equivalents of *two slices of bread*!

Once you can remember that the equivalent (which is how much *complex* carbohydrate you must have every meal—30 grams) is 1 cup of rice or pasta, 2 medium potatoes, 15 French fries, 1 English muffin, ⅔ cup of corn, 1 cup of cooked cereal, etc., you can go anywhere, eat in any restaurant and be perfectly safe. We are assuming you will not only eat your two-slices-of-bread equivalent per meal but another 10 or 20 grams of carbohydrate as well.

Your body cannot distinguish between rice or bread or beans. Or, from the fruit list, it doesn't know the difference between strawberries, grapefruit or blueberries. It only knows it is getting so many grams of complex or simple carbohydrates. Interchange the foods on each list as you like and your body won't care.

Planning Your Meals

To plan meals, there is only one rule: *40 to 50 grams of carbohydrate, with at least 30 grams coming from the starch list.* There's no need to count right down to the very last gram—*approximately* 40 or 50 is sufficient. This makes it very simple. If you can remember the national anthem, you will soon remember the values of the foods you usually eat.

Do not save carbohydrates from one meal to another. Eat your full allotment at each meal or you may run into low-sugar trouble.

Eat about the same number of grams of carbohydrate every day (the only exception: when you plan unusually heavy exercise or nonexercise. See Chapter 5). This is most important for insulin-users, not so critical for those on oral agents, and usually matters not at all if you are diet-controlled. Dosages of insulin are designed to correspond to your food intake. If your carbohydrate intake changes, you will suffer from too much insulin or too little.

Let's start with breakfast.

BREAKFAST

We will assume you eat the typical American breakfast, but you may make your own choices as long as you avoid simple sugars and limit yourself to 40 to 50 grams of other carbohydrates. You only need to do your arithmetic.

For example, you might choose one of the following:

- 3 ounces orange juice, 8 ounces tomato juice or ½ cantaloupe for your breakfast fruit. This accounts for 10 grams of carbohydrate.

Then, adding another 30 grams, choose among these:

- 2 slices toast, 2 halves English muffin, 2 small corn muffins, 2 4-inch pancakes, or 2 slices of French toast. These are worth 15 grams each or 30 grams in all.
- Coffee or tea.

This meal contains about 40 grams of carbohydrate.

If you prefer cereal, substitute ¾ cup (15 grams) plain cold cereal (the amount in the small packages) for the 30 grams of bread, and add 1 cup of milk (12 grams). For ¾ cup of hot cereal, which is more concentrated than cold and worth about 22 grams, add only ½ cup milk.

HELPFUL HINTS

Sometimes you may want ½ banana on your cereal. Then omit the juice or other fruit or drink only a small glass of tomato juice.

If you'd like to add eggs or bacon or any other protein or fat, feel free. The only reason to restrict them is for weight or cholesterol reduction.

The small amount of milk you use in coffee or tea needn't be counted.

Coffee and tea present no special problems for the diabetic. Hypoglycemics, however, sometimes do better with decaffeinated beverages.

Artificial sweeteners may be used (unless you are pregnant).

Obviously you won't use real syrup on your pancakes or French toast. Use only butter or add a *little* dietetic syrup or jelly.

If you take insulin, always be sure to eat the same amount of carbohydrate every morning. Your dose of insulin is predicated on the food you eat. When you eat less, you may have a reaction. When you eat more, you may raise your sugar level. Always have the same kind of breakfast with the same combination of starches and proteins.

To help you plan breakfast, here are the carbohydrate values of 1 cup of some popular cereals. Not included are the sugar-coated varieties, which you must not eat. Note that Grape Nuts are very high in carbohydrate and that the bran cereals are also high. Avoid Grape Nuts and eat only ½ cup of bran cereal or Wheat Chex for your equivalent of two slices of bread.

Cereal (1) cup	*Grams of Carbohydrate*
All-Bran	42.8
Bran Buds	45
Cheerios	16
Cornflakes	18.3
40% Bran Flakes	30
Grape Nuts	92
Grapenut Flakes	31
100% Bran	41.6
Life	30
Nutrigrain	32
Puffed Rice	12.8

Puffed Wheat	10
Raisin Bran	33-45
Rice Krispies	24
Special K	24.6
Shredded Wheat (2 biscuits)	30.4
Total	23
Wheat Chex	46
Wheaties	23

LUNCH AND DINNER

Eat whatever you wish, but try to have a balanced meal. Avoid refined sugars and eat 40 to 50 grams of carbohydrate. Include some vegetables as well as protein, which converts slowly to carbohydrate. If your weight and cholesterol are normal, you may have whatever amount of proteins and fats you are accustomed to eating. If not, see below.

Be sure that every meal includes the equivalent of two slices of bread; or, in other words, two units of the "big" starches found in the 15-gram list. You will need this slowly absorbed carbohydrate to carry you over until your next meal or snack. If all your carbohydrate is taken in the form of fruit or juices (10-gram list), it may throw your blood sugar into a tailspin. On the other hand, always include as well a selection from the 10-gram list to provide the blood sugar you will need in the next couple of hours.

Your lunch may consist of meat or fish, 2 slices of bread or a starch equivalent, one 3-percent vegetable, one 6-percent vegetable. Plus coffee, tea or a diet drink.

For example, perhaps you will choose for lunch

- 3 ounces of meat (0 carbohydrate)
- Salad with lettuce and ½ cup tomatoes (6 grams carbohydrate), with French dressing (1 tablespoon or 3½ grams)
- 2 slices of bread (30 grams)
- ½ cantaloupe (10 grams)

This adds up to 49½ grams of carbohydrate, right in the
ball park.

For dinner, perhaps you will eat

* 3 to 6 ounces of chicken (0 carbohydrate)
* 1 ear of corn (30 grams)
* ½ cup of peas (6 grams)
* ½ grapefruit (10 grams)

You have a total of 46 grams of carbohydrate. Always include a 10-gram fruit at dinner. Many diabetics do better
if they omit fruit from lunch, however.

On special occasions, it is permissible to substitute a
piece of sponge, marble or pound cake for your bread allowance, if the cake weighs the same as a slice of bread.

SNACKS

Diabetics who take insulin should always add two or three
snacks to their three meals so their blood sugar never sinks
too low. Usually, an afternoon and an evening snack are
sufficient, but if you tend to get shaky before lunch, add
one in the morning. Diabetics on diet alone or oral agents
do not need the snacks because they will almost never have
too much insulin in their bloodstreams.

Mid-morning: About 10:30 (if you have had your
breakfast at 7 or 8 A.M.), eat 10 grams of carbohydrate. Perhaps you'll choose 2 graham crackers, or 3 Social Teas, or
a small orange or a glass of milk.

Mid-afternoon: About 3 or 4 P.M., have another 10 or 15
grams of carbohydrate.

Before bed: Eat 15 grams of carbohydrate *plus* some protein before you go to sleep. The protein will slowly convert to carbohydrate during the night, warding off early-
morning insulin reactions.

Suggestions: 1 slice of bread and cheese; a glass of milk;
half a glass of milk with crackers; fruit and cheese; half a
meat sandwich; a scoop of ice cream; peanut butter and
crackers.

Note: the carbohydrate content of the snacks is *in addition to your* 40 to 50 grams per meal. Don't save it from your meals.

FREE FOODS

Along with the 3-percent raw vegetables, these are foods you can eat as you like because they contain very little or no carbohydrate, or they are used in such small amounts as to be insignificant. For example, 1 ounce of soy sauce is only 2.7 grams of carbohydrate.

Bouillon	Mint
Celery salt	Monosodium glutamate
Cinnamon	Mustard
Dietetic candy and gum	Pepper
(up to 5 pieces a day)	Saccharine
Dietetic gelatin (up to	Sour or unsweetened dill
1 cup a day)	pickles
Dietetic jams and jellies	Soy sauce
Garlic	Sugar-free sodas
Herbs	Tartar sauce
Horseradish	Vinegar
Lemon	Worcestershire sauce
Mayonnaise	

If You Want to Lose Weight

To turn this easy carbohydrate-counting diabetic diet into a weight-loss diet, all you have to do is limit the amount of proteins and fats you consume. Remember that with a weight loss many adult diabetics can "lose" their disease for years, maybe forever. Others can cut down on their insulin or oral agent requirements. Sometimes the loss of only a few pounds is enough to increase the number of insulin receptors so that your available insulin is now adequate without outside help.

Do not cut back on your 40 to 50 grams of carbohydrate per meal or your snacks. These are essential to your health. Besides, they are not nearly so fattening as fats and almost all protein foods (most of which have a high percentage of fat), a fact which continues to amaze people who have heard all their lives that bread and potatoes put on weight. What puts on weight is too many calories. Fats and the majority of protein foods contain many more calories than starches.

To lose weight, eat very little fat (butter, cream, margarine, oil, cream cheese, nuts, etc.) and stay away from fried foods. Limit your meat or fish portion to 3 ounces at lunch and dinner. You will now have (including your allotted carbohydrates) a 1,000-calorie diet. Remember, you must eat enough carbohydrate to provide the body's essential fuel and prevent acidosis, so *do not* lower your allotment. If you wish to lose more slowly, you may eat 3 ounces of meat or fish for lunch and 6 ounces for dinner.

If you take insulin, you cannot cut your usual calories without adjusting your dose. So, before you go on a diet, discuss it with your doctor. This is important.

If you take oral agents, you probably won't require a change in dosage, but talk it over with your doctor before beginning your new regime.

If you are on diet alone, you have no problem.

Here is what 3 ounces (about 217 calories) of meat or fish amounts to:

Lean beef:	Hamburger	1 large patty
	Sliced beef	2 slices, 4″ x 4″ x ¼″ each
	Stew	½ cup meat
	Steak	1 small steak
Lamb:	Roast lamb	2 slices, 3″ x 3″ x ½″
	Chop	2 ribs
	Stew	½ cup meat
Liver:		2 slices, 3″ x 3″ x ¼″

Pork:	Chop	1 large chop
	Roast pork	1 slice, 3″ x 3″ x ¼″
Veal:	Chop	1 medium chop, ½″ thick
	Roast veal	1 slice, 3″ x 3″ x ¼″
Chicken:	Broiler	½ small broiler
	Roast	3 slices, 3″ x 3″ x ¼″, or
		1 leg and 1 slice
Turkey:	Roast	2 slices, 4″ x 3″ x ¼″
Fish:	Fresh halibut,	1 slice, 3″ x 3″ x 1″
	cod, salmon,	
	perch, bass,	
	trout	
	Tuna fish	¾ cup (water packed)

For each ounce of meat, substitutions are:

1 slice American cheese
2 strips bacon
2 ounces creamed cottage
    cheese
1 medium egg

1 ounce fish
1 tablespoon peanut butter
5 shrimp, oysters, clams,
    or scallops

How Many Calories Do We Need?

To maintain your weight just where it is, most adults require 10 calories per pound, plus 3 calories per pound for little activity, 5 calories per pound for moderate exertion and 10 calories per pound for strenuous exertion, every day.

In addition, pregnant women require an additional 300 calories a day and those who are breast-feeding need an extra 500 calories a day.

Watching Your Cholesterol Level

If tests show that the cholesterol level of your blood is higher than normal, then it would be wise to make some changes in your diet, eliminating some of the fats. Although controversy rages over whether what you eat has much effect on these fatlike substances which are normal components of the blood and other body tissue, research has shown that a high level of some of these substances is correlated with a higher incidence of heart disease.

Diet can often reduce an abnormally high level, so we recommend that you try. It helps to remember that fat has 250 calories an ounce, or 9 per gram—twice the calories of carbohydrate or protein.

Avoid the foods that contain animal fat and are hard, such as cheese or butter. Cut back on fatty meats, eggs, shellfish, liver and other organ meats. Though most liquid fats are made from vegetables and are unsaturated, some, such as coconut or palm oil, should be crossed off your list, and others, such as cottonseed oil, limited. Use soft tub margarine. When margarine is hardened into bars, it becomes partially saturated. Many people are lucky because they can eat all the "high-cholesterol" foods such as meat and eggs they want without affecting their cholesterol levels. They are born with more lipoprotein lipase, the enzyme that keeps their cholesterol under control. A drug called Atromid S was once widely used to reduce cholesterol, but there are indications that it may cause gallstones. If you do take this drug, however, *be sure* your doctor is aware that you are a diabetic. It may exaggerate the effects of oral agents.

Fast Foods: Safe for Us?

In today's hectic world, families no longer eat home-cooked meals every night and lunches are often taken on the run. For this reason, we should all know the carbohydrate values of the ready-to-eat food we may encounter.

Take, for example, hamburgers: A hamburger roll, top and bottom, is the equivalent of 2 slices of bread (30 grams of carbohydrate). The meat within is your protein. Do not overdo the catsup, since 1 tablespoon equals about 4½ grams of carbohydrate. The dressing also contains some sugar, but a small amount won't matter. Skip the French fries unless you are exercising strenuously or doing some heavy manual labor and need the extra grams of carbohydrate (15 French fries equal 30 grams). Forget the cola (except sugarless) and the milk shake. They are not for you.

As for pizza parlors, remember 1 slice of pizza equals almost 2 slices of bread or 30 grams.

Now let's consider "fish 'n' chips." The batter contains some carbohydrate, so judge the thickness and perhaps have two pieces of fish rather than three. Fifteen French fries would be the equivalent of 2 slices of bread. Go easy on the coleslaw because it probably contains sugar.

MORE HELPFUL HINTS

• A banana is a banana, whether it is green, yellow or purple, and contains the same amount of carbohydrate even if it is called a plantain.

• Fructose is not for you because it is converted very quickly into glucose and raises your blood sugar accordingly.

• Apple, pineapple, grape and prune juice, even "unsweetened," are no-nos because their sugars are much too rapidly absorbed into the bloodstream. Apples, too, frequently affect glucose tolerance adversely and should be avoided by most diabetics and hypoglycemics. A decent-size apple often contains 30 grams of rapidly metabolized sugar.

• For the same reason, take care with applesauce, even if it is unsweetened. It is loaded with natural sugar.

• It won't help you a bit to toast your bread or eat it stale. It still retains its carbohydrate content and has merely lost its water content.

• Common pitfalls are dried fruits—raisins, prunes, dried figs, pineapple, apricots, etc. They are *very* high in sugar.

• Soups frequently are the cause of a blood-sugar disaster. One patient had a very erratic pattern, with reactions one day, high sugars the next, and decided she was a brittle diabetic. It turned out the brittleness was in the soup she was eating. She ate lunch at the same restaurant every day, always ordering the soup of the day. The thick soups—barley, lentil, pea or minestrone vegetable soups—made her sugar soar. All of these soups contain astonishing concentrations of carbohydrate, too much for one meal. The days she had plain chicken soup were the days she had insulin reactions.

The soups you can eat without worry include: chicken, onion, some tomato soups, mushroom, celery, zucchini, gazpacho, cucumber—the plain soups.

If you eat creamed soup or chowders made with flour, omit one of your two units of starch for that meal. The same applies for heavy gravies.

Borscht, which is made from beets that are high in sugar, should be crossed off your list.

• Remember sugars and simple carbohydrates are often needed to fight off insulin reactions, but the complex carbohydrates plus protein are best if you have time and they work for you.

• When you are planning to get involved in heavy exercise or manual labor, take extra carbohydrates before you begin. Some people need 60 or 70 grams per meal to compensate for strenuous physical activity.

• On the other hand, if you are suddenly not getting your accustomed exercise—if you are in bed with a broken leg—you will require more insulin and maybe less carbohydrate. Only your urine or blood tests will give you the answer.

• Once you know the general rules of your diet, then apply your common sense. For example, you go to a Chinese restaurant and start with two egg rolls. The coating on the egg rolls is probably equivalent to a slice of bread (15 grams of starch). Now eat the main course of fish or meat with vegetables, and you can still have the equivalent of another slice. That means ½ cup of rice. The carbohydrate value of Chinese soups is negligible if you avoid those containing sugar, such as sweet and sour. For dessert, you can have fruit or a couple of fortune cookies.

Using the same common sense, you can eat without fear in any restaurant. When you go out for an Italian meal, consider a small side order of spaghetti to be equal to 2 slices of bread or 30 grams of carbohydrate. Skip the bread and the bread sticks. Eat the main course and a salad.

• Avoid "instant" breakfasts and yogurt containing *anything*. The fruits and flavors that are added are usually sugar-laden.

• A few slices of onions on a hamburger or in a salad won't hurt you, but remember that 5 or 6 pearl (or larger) onions in a stew equals about 8 grams of carbohydrate. Proceed with caution. The same with tomatoes—a big ripe tomato that tastes so good right out of the garden can throw your sugar way off.

More Pitfalls

There are so many sugar traps lurking around that it might be helpful to be aware of a few more common pitfalls. These are foods you may never have suspected of containing inordinate amounts of sugar, but could throw your glucose tolerance for a real loop.

- The most popular brand of catsup contains 29 percent sugar. A tablespoon on your hamburger can be tolerated, though.
- If you use a lot of Sweet 'n' Low, an artificial sweetener, be aware that one package contains 1 gram of sugar, so 4 to 5 packages throughout the day will add up to a lump of sugar.
- According to *Consumer Reports*, many processed foods contain a lot of hidden sugar. For example, high in sugar value are Coffee-mate nondairy creamer (65.4 percent), and Quaker Oats 100 Percent Natural Cereal (24 percent). Hamburger Helper for Lasagna has 23 percent added sugar; Jell-O is over 82 percent sugar; Shake 'n Bake Barbecue Chicken Coating is 50.9 percent sugar. Learn to read labels before eating concocted foods.
- Other foods with high sugar content include All-Bran, 100% Bran, Bran Buds, Raisin Bran and, of course, all sugar-coated cereals.
- Beware of "milk imitations," such as nondairy creamers, fake whipped cream, etc. Most of them contain sugar as well as a long list of chemicals. Always ask for fresh milk for your coffee.
- Never substitute "fruit drinks" for fruit juice. They are not only mostly water, which you can get almost free at home, but they are made with lots of sugar.
- Always take responsibility for your own food. Even hospital dietitians have been known to serve the wrong foods to diabetics, so you must monitor your food just as you do at home, counting your carbohydrates. For example, apple juice, prune juice and grape juice are frequently found on the hospital breakfast tray. These may not be bowls of granulated sugar nor are they chocolate cookies, but they are still not right for you because they contain too much quickly absorbed sugar that will surely swamp you.

Perhaps you'll be offered 8 ounces of orange juice (almost 27 grams of quick sugar) as part of your breakfast. It is doubtful you can handle that amount of quick sugar at one time. Or you may be given too many starches at once— bread, corn, potatoes, all in the same meal, for example— which will far exceed your carbohydrate limits, especially when you are in bed and getting no exercise, and even more especially when you will probably get fruit for dessert and perhaps a 6-percent vegetable.

Don't eat foods you know are not right for you, even if they arrive on your tray. Argue every debatable item with your doctor and/or the dietician. Remember you are not exempt from your usual eating pattern just because you are in the hospital. As a matter of fact, now is the time to watch your food more carefully than usual because your illness may make you especially sensitive to fluctuating blood-sugar levels.

• Cottage cheese, pot cheese, cream cheese, sour cream and other cheeses, though they are milk products, cannot be substituted for milk or yogurt as part of your carbohydrate allotment, but you can include them in your diet as you wish as a protein. No restrictions unless you wish to lose weight. While milk contains about equal amounts of carbohydrate, protein and fat, these foods have little carbohydrate compared to their protein and fat.

• Breaded foods count toward your total carbohydrates. Omit the equivalent of 1 slice of bread (15 grams) when you eat them.

• Read labels! Some "health" foods, such as Tofutti, contain honey or other forms of sugar and will raise blood sugar in a hurry.

Spicing Up Your Salad

• Salad dressings can present a problem because some of them contain considerable carbohydrate. But if you use just a tiny amount, you can get away with most varieties.

When in doubt, make your own dressing or flavor your salad with wine vinegar or lemon, plus spices. You may add oil unless you are trying to lose weight. It contains no carbohydrate.

To help you, here are the carbohydrate values of a few prepared salad dressings.

Salad Dressing: 1 tablespoon	*Grams of Carbohydrate*
Lawry's Caesar	.5
Wish-Bone Caesar	.6
Hellmann's French	2.9
Wish-Bone Garlic	3.6
Lawry's Green Goddess	.7
Wish-Bone Green Goddess	1.2
Lawry's Hawaiian	5.8
Hellman's Italian	.8
Lawry's with cheese	4.7
Mayonnaise	Less than 1
Wish-Bone Russian	7.2
Tahitian Isle	7.2
Thousand Island	Under 3

Though most salad dressings do not contain much carbohydrate, they are usually laden with calories, a fact to keep in mind if you are overweight. Most low-calorie dressings contain less (some much less) than 3 grams of carbohydrate per tablespoon. A few, such as Wish-Bone's low-calorie Russian and French, contain more (5.4 and 3.3).

Timing Your Food

If you take insulin, *when* you eat is just as important as *what* you eat. *All* diabetics and hypoglycemics should space out their carbohydrate intake throughout the day so that there won't be high peaks and low valleys in blood-sugar levels. But if you take insulin, you must also worry about reactions. It's important that you eat at specified times because, like a time bomb, the hormone acts at fixed hours of the day. If you don't have food in anticipation of these periods of high insulin action, you will have reactions.

Never skip a meal or a planned snack. Do not delay your meals. If you are going to a party and know dinner will be served later than your usual mealtime, eat 30 grams of your carbohydrate at your usual time. Then, when you get to the dinner party, skip those 30 grams of carbohydrate (rolls, potatoes, pilaf, etc.) and eat the main course, salad, vegetables and fruit for dessert. Do not take a chance that you may last until your hostess or the restaurant serves you. Plan ahead or you'll spoil the whole affair for everyone.

To Fast or Not to Fast

Fast days such as Yom Kippur can complicate the lives of diabetics who take insulin. If you are controlled by diet alone, fasting is no problem. If you take oral drugs, it is no problem either, but it might be best to skip your pill in the morning and take it before the evening meal that breaks the fast.

For insulin-users, fasting is much trickier, and you would be wise not to try it. Surely your need for food when you are diabetic will not alter the effectiveness of your prayers. Better to bend the traditional rules than to encounter a medical emergency.

If fasting is very important to you, however, it can be done. Suppose you normally take 10 Regular and 30 units of Intermediate insulin in the morning. If today is a fast day, take no insulin in the morning, have no breakfast or lunch. Suppose the day goes by and you remain asymptomatic. Check your urine before dinner. If you find you have high sugar (almost a sure bet), do *not* take your usual morning dose. Take more Regular (to compensate for the higher-than-normal sugar) and less Intermediate (because you don't want it to last through the next day). For example: 20 Regular and 20 Intermediate.

But suppose, without insulin, breakfast and lunch, you begin having symptoms of high sugar and acidosis—frequent urination, thirst, etc. *Do not wait* for dinner. Break the fast *immediately*. Start eating and take your insulin, again increasing your Regular to take care of the high sugar and cutting back on your Intermediate insulin.

Comments on "Cheating"

There are very few perfect people in this world, and diabetics are no more likely to be among them than anyone else. It is a rare diabetic who doesn't cheat on his prescribed diet once in a while. This is not the end of the world and you shouldn't feel too guilty about it. But it is *not* a good idea to fall off your diet regularly because, if you do, your control will automatically be poor and you will be subject to all the ills and complications that befall poorly controlled diabetics.

For insulin-taking people who cheat occasionally, it is possible to compensate for a binge by taking a urine test after the event and taking a few extra units of Regular insulin if you see very high sugar. The best way to cheat, however, is to do your forbidden eating before you set off on a program of strenuous exercise, when you may need extra carbohydrates anyway. For example, if you are going to the movies, don't overindulge at dinner. But if your plans include disco dancing, you can probably plan on burning off the excess carbohydrate before the night is out.

Fiber Diets: Good for Diabetics

According to recent research, increased fiber in your diet can improve your glucose tolerance. Some fiber foods, such as pectin, guar and oat bran, are water-soluble. They delay absorption of carbohydrates by trapping them within themselves and releasing them slowly. Because of the delay, less sugar enters the bloodstream immediately after a meal, avoiding an overload. This kind of fiber also seems to lower the level of cholesterol in the blood.

Other fibers, such as cellulose, lignin and wheat bran, are not water-soluble. They pass through the digestive system quickly, taking other foods along with them, giving the intestines less opportunity to absorb carbohydrates. These also soften the stool and add bulk to it.

The canes, roots and tubers that, before we became so "civilized," once constituted the major part of mankind's daily food have been replaced by a diet high in animal proteins and fats as well as grain cereals which have lost most of their fiber content in the milling process. The typical Western diet includes only about four grams of crude fiber a day. In some less-developed countries it makes up 30 grams of the daily diet, and is associated with lower incidences of diabetes, diverticulitis, appendicitis, hemorrhoids and cancer of the colon. On the other hand, except for lignin found in strawberries and pears, it increases flatulence (gas).

Fiber is undigestible, unabsorbable plant material and is not found in meat or fish. It leaves the digestive system in much the same form it went in and has virtually no caloric value. Nevertheless, it plays a number of vital roles in the digestive process. It is found chiefly in whole grains, nuts and beans, fruits and vegetables, especially those with edible skins and seeds. It does not matter whether these foods are eaten raw, cooked, frozen or canned.

Should you, a diabetic, eat a high-fiber diet? More fiber certainly will not hurt you and it may well give you an extra little edge. It won't cure your diabetes, but it is possible it may tip the scales in your favor. So, the answer is yes. If you are on diet alone or oral agents, you may find that your available insulin is more effective with more fiber. And if you take insulin you may require a little less of the medication. It isn't, however, a cure-all; there is a limit to the amount of fiber you can eat safely, because these fiber foods are mainly high-starch compounds that take time to be broken down but nonetheless are absorbed as carbohydrate at some time during their metabolism. Among the fiber foods, peas and baked beans have been found to raise blood sugar more than the others.

Important: Remember to include the fiber foods in your 40 to 50 grams of carbohydrate per meal. Dried beans and bran cereals, for example, tend to be high-carbohydrate foods. Two tablespoons of miller's bran equal about 15 grams of carbohydrate, and you must account for it in your total allotment. Sprinkled over a low-carbohydrate cereal (¾ cup or 15 grams), you now have 30 grams. Add a half cup of milk, and your total is about 36 grams of carbohydrate, leaving you room for only about 10 more grams for that particular meal.

To get more fiber into your diet, you should eat:

• Whole-grain breads and cereals, especially whole bran or bran-containing foods, or guar, a substance made from the cluster bean and available in health food stores.

• Nuts and seeds.

• Vegetables such as artichokes, broccoli, cabbage, cauliflower, Brussels sprouts, corn, peas, peppers, beans, cucumber, carrots.

• Fruits such as strawberries, blueberries, grapefruit and raw pears.

• Leguminous dried beans—butter, haricot, kidney, soy, lentils, black-eyed or chickpeas, etc.

"Fiber breads" may be added to the list. Check the carbohydrate content of each slice so you can be sure to eat a sufficient number of grams.

Caution: Sometimes the absorption of some important trace minerals, such as calcium, zinc, iron and magnesium, is inhibited when you consume too much fiber. Their absorption, along with that of glucose, may be decreased. So don't go overboard. Eat well-balanced meals that happen to include sufficient fiber.

Some people prefer to get their extra fiber by sprinkling miller's bran into their food. Fruits and vegetables are a much more nutritious alternative, and it is best to get your fiber the natural way, by eating properly.

If you are not accustomed to much fiber in your diet, work up to a higher amount gradually. If you notice too much gas or bloating, cut back until you have adjusted. Your body probably will become accustomed to it in a few weeks.

Don't eat your fiber between meals, or it won't have food to act upon. Eat it with your other food.

Do You Need Vitamin Supplements?

This is an age of megavitamins, and much controversy exists over the need for vitamins and minerals in addition to a balanced diet. Though most medical experts do not think anyone who eats a wide variety of nourishing foods requires supplements, there is some thought that a few of them may be helpful to diabetics. Let's go down the list.

Vitamin B_1: This is a vitamin I recommend to my patients with diabetic neuropathy and about 80 percent of them show some improvement or even complete relief when they take it regularly in daily 50 to 100 mg doses. It is especially helpful for neuropathy (pain or burning) of the feet. Sometimes injections of vitamin B_{12} also help.

Vitamin B_6: Because this is thought to increase glucose tolerance in pregnant woman, a supplement of 25 mgs a day is recommended during pregnancy.

Vitamin C: Though there is no real scientific proof that it is so, it has been proclaimed that large doses of vitamin C are effective in fighting off numerous ailments, including colds. Many doctors recommend C supplements because they believe it strengthens the capillary walls of the eyes and prevents retinopathy (diabetic eye changes).

We recommend you add 50 mgs of vitamin C to your daily menu.

Remember, however, that very large doses of vitamin C can interfere with the results of urine tests, perhaps giving you false readings. If you take a large amount, you may get a false positive when you use Clinitest, or a false negative when you use one of the strip tests (see Chapter 8). If you seem to be getting unreliable test results, stop the vitamin C for a few days and see if your results are different. Or change your testing methods.

Vitamin E: This vitamin, called "the vitamin in search of a disease," is claimed to improve circulation, retard the destruction of polyunsaturated fats and protect against arteriosclerosis. Again, no definite proof is available, but there is a chance vitamin E may help prevent some degenerative processes.

Don't forget that wheat germ, a favorite source of vitamin E, adds a lot of carbohydrate and must be accounted for in your diet. Two tablespoons count as 15 grams (1 starch).

Chromium is needed for good glucose metabolism, but if you eat a balanced diet you will probably have sufficient chromium without taking supplements. Deficiencies of this metal seldom occur except in the elderly. Rich dietary sources include brewer's yeast and liver.

Calcium supplements are recommended for anyone who

does not drink milk, eat milk products or get regular exercise, and they are especially important for postmenopausal women.

Magnesium is in short supply in some diabetics with severe retinopathy, but is not yet known whether adding magnesium salts to your diet will prevent eye changes. Natural sources: cereals, nuts, beans, meats.

Zinc is required for normal growth and development, and some research has shown that, given orally in 200 mg doses, it helps heal diabetic ulcers. It is found naturally in green leafy vegetables, fruits, whole-grain breads, and meat. Don't overdose yourself—too much zinc will cause nausea.

Note: There is no difference, except in the price, between natural and synthetic vitamins.

Sweeteners: Blessing or Danger?

Saccharine and aspartame make life a little bit sweeter for people who can't eat sugar, and, from what we know now, there is no reason not to use them. A few years ago, experiments with rats showed an increased incidence of bladder tumors among second-generation rats fed the equivalent of 800 diet sodas a day. Saccharine was promptly removed from many homes and hospitals as a result. However, subsequent research on people has completely failed to show the correlation between the sweetener and cancer, while coffee and cigarettes have both been definitely implicated in a rise in bladder cancer.

As for aspartame (Nutrasweet and Equal), it has been approved by the F.D.A. though its safety is still questioned by consumer groups at this writing.

It is always best for pregnant women to avoid any artificial chemicals or unnecessary drugs on the chance that they may have an adverse effect on the developing fetus, so they should not use sweeteners. For other diabetics and hypoglycemics, however, they are a much better choice than sugar and keep you from feeling like second-class citizens. Children, especially, need to feel they are not being totally deprived of the goodies their friends consume so freely.

The Lure of "Dietetic" Foods

Just because a package food (usually very expensive) is labeled "dietetic," it does not mean it is good for diabetics. Though no refined sugar has been included, it may still contain much more carbohydrate than you can handle. Take, for example, dietetic apple pie. Though it may be sweetened artificially, it still has a crust and plenty of apples, and you can exceed your limit without added sugar. On the other hand, you may be able to get away with a piece of dietetic blueberry pie occasionally because it contains a lower sugar content than apple pie, and the natural sugar is not as quickly absorbed. Count the crust as two slices of bread or 30 grams of carbohydrate, and substitute the blueberries for your fruit at dinner. Guide yourself by your urine or blood tests.

Though such items as water-packed canned fruits, dietetic jellies and gelatin desserts can perk up your menu, many modified foods still contain too much sugar, honey or syrup for you (though perhaps in smaller amounts than the usual recipe) as well as carbohydrates in other forms.

In general, foods called "noncaloric" or those containing only a few (under 10) calories per serving are safe, eaten in limited amounts. For example, you can safely eat small amounts of dietetic jam or candy. But stay away from dietetic cookies, cakes, chocolates, sherbets, breads and custards, as well as liquid nondairy creamers, dietetic dinners and diet bars. Unless you are a chemist, the listed ingredients of most processed dietetic foods are impossible to interpret correctly.

Faked Out by Fructose

Once proclaimed to be the answer to a diabetic's dream of a "good" sugar, fructose has not lived up to its expectations. Though this kind of sugar does not require insulin for its metabolism, it converts to glucose in the body and can raise blood-sugar levels just like any of its sugary relatives. The more deficient in insulin you are, the quicker the conversion.

Sorbitol and mannitol, both sugar alcohols, are also converted to glucose, but more slowly. You may be able to handle these in tiny amounts, though some people respond to them with cramps and diarrhea.

Learn to Read Labels

Sugar comes in many disguises. Beware of any ingredients that end in "-ose" or "-tol." These are usually just plain sugar. For example: dextrose, lactose, sorbitol. Sometimes labels list several varieties of sugar with different names, such as: dextrose, fructose, glucose, sucrose, sorbitol, mannitol, lactose, disaccharide, corn syrup, corn sugar, corn syrup solids, honey, molasses, maltose. Watch out for all of them! Add a few together in one food and you come up with a high percentage of sugar, more than you can cope with.

Recent legislation requires that the ingredients of most foods be listed on the label, and also the amounts in grams of carbohydrates, proteins and fats, according to serving size. Use this information to plan your 40 to 50 grams of carbohydrate per meal.

No Smoking Allowed!

We all know by now that smoking is hazardous to everyone's health. For diabetics, who already have a tendency toward vascular disease, smoking is even more dangerous. Smoking affects the coronary blood vessels as well as the smaller vessels in the legs and feet, constricting them, reducing circulation and affecting the ability of any damaged tissues to heal. In addition, diabetics, especially if they are not in good control, have less oxygen in their tissues than other people. Smoking raises the blood level of carbon monoxide, thus adding to that oxygen deficit even if you smoke filtered cigarettes. Smoking is also known to increase a tendency toward retinopathy.

If you are a smoker, do yourself an enormous favor and quit.

Smoking "Pot" and Doing Other Drugs

Though there are conflicting reports about the effects of marijuana on mind and body, it is certain that this drug is not a good idea for you. For one thing, it can mask insulin reactions so you may not recognize that you need immediate food. For another thing, it distorts your sense of time so that you may not eat on schedule. And it may set off the "munchies," a craving for sweets that has obvious drawbacks.

Amphetamines (uppers) are stimulants that can raise or lower your blood sugar unexpectedly. Narcotics (heroin and cocaine) can affect the blood sugar by altering absorption of sugar. So, for these reasons, as well as many others, don't try to get your kicks from drugs.

Ginseng, a Cure-all?

Ginseng, a root popular in the Orient, is said to cure many ills, but don't try it if you are diabetic. Ginseng has a steroidlike effect that may raise blood sugar, cause ulcers and enlarge male breasts, and may well be damaging for anyone.

Alcohol—What Does It Do to You?

Being a diabetic (or hypoglycemic) doesn't mean you must give up all your former bad habits. You don't have to go on the wagon and become a teetotaler. On the other hand, you must be a "sensible" drinker. A drink or two a day won't hurt you, if you are in good control and remember a few facts. Actually, alcohol in moderation is thought to raise high-density lipoproteins (the "good" fat) and decrease chances of heart attacks.

Alcohol has no food value and contains no carbohydrates or other nutrients, though it does add calories to your daily diet. An ounce of whiskey, for example, contains about 85 calories. *Sweet* alcoholic drinks, however, do contain some sugar.

Here are some guidelines to follow:

• Never drink on an empty stomach. Alcohol blocks the process called gluconeogenesis, the formation of glucose from protein and its release from the liver when your blood sugar is too low. Without food, you risk having a severe hypoglycemic reaction if you are on insulin. When you drink before meals, eat hors d'oeuvre but be sure to count them as part of your meal's allotment of carbohydrate.

• Never have more than two drinks, even with food. You may not be able to recognize a reaction or distinguish it from intoxication. (Nor may the police, if you are pulled over for erratic driving.)

• Don't change your insulin dose or diet to allow for your alcoholic drinks.

• Watch out for the "Antabuse effect" if you take Diabinese, an oral agent. Alcohol will sometimes cause surface blood vessels to dilate, producing marked facial flushing, plus a choking sensation and maybe a headache.

• Sweet drinks do contain carbohydrate. So do the hors d'oeuvre that usually accompany drinking. Avoid sweet wines, stout, cider, ginger beer, port, liqueurs and cordials. Don't drink sweet mixers such as tonic unless they are sugar-free, and remember that the orange juice in a screwdriver, for example, counts toward your total allotment of quick carbohydrate for that meal.

• A drink before dinner or a glass or two of dry wine with dinner is considered permissible for most diabetics and hypoglycemics. The acceptable list includes: Scotch, rye, whiskey, bourbon, tequila, brandy, rum, gin, vodka and light dry wine.

• To slip an occasional beer or ale into your life, omit one slice of bread or a fruit at dinner to make up for it. There are about 10 grams of carbohydrate in 8 ounces of beer.

• Don't get excited if your hostess serves food cooked with wine. The carbohydrate addition is negligible and most of the alcohol is lost in the cooking. If you take Diabinese and you suffer from the "Antabuse effect," however, then you must be more careful. Ask questions before you eat.

Rating the Popular Diets

Now for a brief discussion of some of the diets that are popular today. Are they good for you?

AMOUNTS OF CARBOHYDRATE, ALCOHOL AND CALORIES IN ALCOHOLIC DRINKS*

Alcoholic Drinks	Amount	Total Grams	Grams of Carbohydrate	Grams of Alcohol	Calories (Approx.)
Whiskey—Bourbon, Irish, Rye and Scotch	1 brandy glass (1 oz.)	30	none	10½–13	75–85
Brandy, Gin and Rum	1 brandy glass (1 oz.)	30	none	10½–13	75–90
Liqueurs and Cordials	1 cordial glass (⅔ oz.)	20	4–10	4–7	50–80
Malt, liquors—ale, beer, porter and stout	1 glass (8 oz.)	240	7–14	7–14	80–150
WINES					
Sweet, domestic	1 wine glass (3½ oz.)	100	8–14	13–15	140–165
Sweet, imported	1 wine glass (3½ oz.)	100	3–20	10½–18	110–175
Dry, domestic	1 wine glass (3½ oz.)	100	½–4	10–11	75–90
Dry, imported	1 wine glass (3½ oz.)	100	½–3	8–14	60–110
CIDER					
Sweet	1 glass (8 oz.)	240	25	trace	100
Hard (fermented)	1 wine glass (3½ oz.)	100	1	5	40

* From *The Joslin Clinic Diabetes Teaching Guide*, compiled by George P. Kozak, M.D., Joslin Clinic, Joslin Diabetes Foundation, Boston, Mass.

• *The Pritikin Diet* is low in fats, cholesterol, protein and refined sugars. It is high in starches and complex carbohydrates such as grains, vegetables and fruits. It recommends exercise.

If you can follow this complicated eating regime, it will probably be good for you with some modifications. Though it is yet to be proven as a way to prevent heart disease or cure diabetes or anything else, it is obviously a healthy diet. And the recommended exercise should, of course, be part of every diabetic's life style. Physical acitity lowers blood sugar and improves glucose tolerance dramatically.

If you decide to try the Pritikin diet, watch out for highly concentrated sources of sugar as well as carbohydrates that are absorbed much too quickly to be safe. These include honey, certain nuts, raisins, dates, Grape Nuts, apple juice, beets, heavy soups, sweet potatoes, super amounts of beans and 6-percent vegetables. Count the carbohydrates and have no more than your allotment of 40 to 50 grams per meal.

• *Vegetarian* diets have become popular in America, among diabetics as well as the rest of the population. Will they work for you? They can, *if* you consult a dietician for advice before you begin. You must eat a diet balanced in carbohydrates, fats and proteins and this is not a simple matter if you don't eat meat or fish.

It is recommended that you do not follow a strict vegetarian diet, eliminating all animal foods and eating only plants. To get the needed supply of protein, strict vegetarians consume exotic combinations of vegetables and grains that will far exceed the levels of carbohydrate that are safe for you. Besides, this diet puts you in danger of deficiencies of important vitamins and minerals.

If your diet allows fish, eggs and/or dairy products, being a vegetarian is not quite as tricky, though tricky it remains. The protein plant foods used to supplement fish and dairy foods are very high in carbohydrate. For example, it takes only ⅛ cup of cooked lentil, mung, pinto, red beans or chickpeas, or ¼ cup of soy beans, to equal about 15 grams of carbohydrate.

You must take care not to consume too many grams of carbohydrate at any one time, especially not too many of the quickly absorbed variety. The usual large amounts of carbohydrate in a vegetarian diet can easily cause problems with your blood-sugar level, though the increased fiber may give you a little more leeway.

• *The popular fast-loss diets:* We would all like to lose weight quickly when we are too heavy, not just a pound or two a week as our doctors and the more sensible weight-loss diets suggest. Are quick diets safe for you?

They may be safe for mild diabetics if you stay on them for only two weeks at the outside, if your health is good, if you are under medical supervision and if you have your own doctor's approval.

Let's take, for example, the Scarsdale Diet. If you are a diabetic controlled by diet alone, you should have no worries if you stay away from certain fruits that are loaded with natural sugar.

If you take oral agents, you will have to make certain adjustments. On some days, the diet provides more rapidly absorbed carbohydrate than your body can possibly cope with. You can try the diet as written and see by your urine tests whether your sugar goes too high after, say, the Tuesday and Saturday lunches, which are all fruit. If it does, you must revert to the amounts *and* the kinds of carbohydrates recommended in this book—40 to 50 grams, with 30 of them from the starch list. You will still lose weight.

If you take insulin, you will almost surely run into trouble on the days when you eat little starch, though lowering your insulin dose on those days may help. This is very risky, however, so in your case it is best to skip the diet and other quick diets altogether.

All diabetics should follow the suggested recipes included in the Scarsdale book with caution. Some contain such sugar-loaded foods as prune juice and pineapple chunks.

Other popular diets—the quickies—that feature high protein and low carbohydrate can be dangerous too, though if you are on diet alone you can probably get away with them for a short time. More severe diabetics cannot because these diets are designed to burn fat and produce a state of acidosis, just what you must avoid. Remember, acidosis inhibits the action of insulin and can put you right in the hospital.

• *Low-salt diets:* If your doctor has told you to lower your salt intake, then you must avoid every food high in salt even if it is otherwise permissible. Dry cereals, for example, tend to be high in salt as are processed meats and canned vegetables.

• *Low-potassium diets:* Certain fruits, such as figs, pineapple, apples, raisins and prunes, that are recommended for kidney disease are not recommended for you because their sugar is too readily absorbed. Stay with the fruits that have low potassium *and* are permissible for you, such as cranberry juice, grapefruit, grapes, peaches, berries, tangerines, pears, plums, watermelon, nectarines.

CARBOHYDRATE VALUES OF POPULAR FOODS*

Food	Amount	Carbohydrate Content (Grams)
Almonds	½ cup, shelled	14
Apple	1 medium, raw	20
Artichoke, boiled	4 oz.	11
Artichoke hearts	5–6 hearts, 3 oz.	22
Anchovies	1 oz.	.1
Avocado	½ fruit	6.4 to 10.8
Bacon	2 slices	.2
Baked beans	½ cup	20–30
Bamboo shoots	Raw, ½ lb.	3.4
Banana	1 small	21
Bean sprouts	½ cup, raw	3
Beans, black	Dry, 4 oz.	69
Beans, green or wax, fresh, boiled	½ cup	3.5
Beans, Italian	½ cup	5
Beans, lima, boiled	½ cup	17–21
Beans, pinto	Dry, ½ cup	61
Beans, lentil	Dry, ½ cup	58
Beans, garbanzo (chickpeas)	Dry, ½ cup	61
Beef pie, frozen	8 oz.	40
Beef, consommé or broth	1 cup	2.7
Beets, cooked	½ cup	7.4
Bread crumbs	1 tbsp.	4.7
Buckwheat groats	1 oz.	21
Cashew nuts	½ cup	20
Catsup	1 tbsp.	4.9
Cheese cake	1/6 of 8" cake	38.8
Chestnuts, fresh, shelled	3 large	10
Chicken pie	8 oz.	50
Chili sauce	1 tbsp.	4.6
Coconut, fresh	½ cup, grated	3.8
Coconut, dried, sweetened	½ cup	23
Cornstarch	1 tbsp.	7
Cracker crumbs, graham	1 cup	76.6
Curry powder	1 tbsp.	4.9
Dates	5	40.5

* Adapted from *Calories and Carbohydrates*, 4th Revised Edition by Barbara Kraus (The New American Library); *Composition of Foods, Agriculture Handbook No. 8* (USDA); *Nutritive Values of American Foods, Agriculture Handbook No. 456* (USDA); and *Joslin Clinic Diabetes Teaching Guide*, compiled by George P. Kozak, M.D.

CARBOHYDRATE VALUES OF POPULAR FOODS

Food	Amount	Carbohydrate Content (Grams)
Eggnog	½ cup	17
Fig, fresh	1, small	7.6
Flour	1 oz.	21
Frankfurter	1	.7
Gefilte fish, canned	1 piece, 4 oz.	4.2
Lasagne, canned	8 oz.	29.7
frozen with meat sauce	7½ oz.	43
Lemon juice, fresh	1 lemon	4
Mango, fresh	1 medium	33.6
Matzoh meal	1 cup	94
Mayonnaise	1 tbsp.	.2
Milk, condensed, sweetened	1 cup	166
Milk, evaporated	1 cup	24
Milk, whole, skim or buttermilk	1 cup	12
Oil		0
Onion, raw, chopped	½ cup	7.5
Papaya	4 oz.	11.3
Peanuts	½ cup, shelled	13
Peanut butter	1 tab.	2–4
Pecans	½ cup shelled	7.9
Pimiento, canned	4 oz.	6.6
Pizza, home baked, with cheese	4 oz.	32
Popcorn, plain	1 cup	10.7
Potato chips	1 oz.	14
Raisins, whole	½ cup	55.7
Ravioli, canned, beef	1 cup	28.3
Relish, hot-dog	1 tbsp.	5
Sandwich spread	1 tbsp.	2.4
Sardines, canned in oil	3 oz.	0
Sesame seeds, dry, whole	1 oz.	6.1
Soybean curd	4 oz.	2.7
Succotash, frozen	½ cup	19
Sugar	1 tbsp.	12.1
Sunflower seeds, hulled	1 oz.	5.6
Sweet potato, peeled	1 medium	38
Tomato, fresh	1 medium	7
Tomato juice	½ cup	5.2
Tomato paste	6 oz.	31
Tomato purée	1 cup	22
Tomato sauce	1 cup	20
Vegetable juice cocktail, canned	4 oz.	4.1
Vegetables, mixed, frozen	½ cup	12

FIVE

Exercise: Essential for Diabetics

Better to hunt in Fields, for Health unbought,
than fee the doctor for a nauseous Draught.
The Wise, for Cure, on exercise depend;
God never made his Work, for Man to mend.

—John Dryden

You have to have buried yourself up to your eyebrows and worn earmuffs not to know that exercise is good for you. Everyone in America today seems to be involved in fitness programs of one variety or another, from yoga to running, and that includes plenty of diabetics. We all know now that regular vigorous exercise strengthens the cardiovascular system, lowers "bad" low-density lipid levels in the blood while raising the "good" high-density fats, tones your muscles, improves your circulation, lowers your blood pressure and heart rate, promotes a sense of well-being and burns off excess weight.

That is quite a list of benefits, but exercise is especially good medicine for most diabetics who, because they have a special tendency toward overweight, poor circulation, high tryglycerides, elevated blood pressure, blood clots and accelerated arteriosclerosis, need all the help they can get.

But exercise does even more for you. It can actually help keep your diabetes under control and lower your insulin requirements. Exercise has been called "invisible insulin," and that's just what it is. The more exercise you get, if you are in good health, the less insulin you are likely to require and the more stable your diabetes will probably be.

Exercise lowers the level of glucose circulating in your bloodstream. Muscles use glucose as their fuel, first consuming whatever is in the blood, then calling on the liver to deliver more from its stores of glycogen, using it faster than it can be produced. Unless this is carried to an extreme, it is obviously a fine feature for a diabetic who has the chronic problem of glucose disposal. There is evidence, too, that this improved glucose tolerance tends to last for a number of hours after exercise, sometimes even through the next day. A young person requires only about 15 or 20 minutes of jogging a day, and an older person only 10 minutes of brisk walking two or three times a day to bring sugar levels down significantly.

With exercise, insulin is also more readily taken up by the body's cells because of an increase in both insulin sensitivity and the actual number of receptors on target cells in muscle, fat and liver tissue. A recent study at Yale University Medical Center demonstrated a 30 percent rise in insulin sensitivity and a 50 percent increase in the number of insulin cell receptors among a group of subjects after a six-week program of daily physical training.

Another study, made in Denmark, shows a similar increase in glucose tolerance and insulin intake among diabetics who exercised every morning.

If you are ready for another documented reason to get

exercise, here it is: regular physical activity can reduce your risk of developing the diabetic eye changes called ret-inopathy and other vascular diabetic complications. Many diabetics have an abnormal tendency toward "sticky" blood platelets, platelets that clump together and form clots. Research at the University of California Medical Center in San Francisco found that, for both juvenile-type diabetics and normal individuals, there is a significant drop in this stickiness with exercise, an effect that tends to last many hours.

Duke University researchers who measured the biochem-ical response to a blockage of veins in healthy adults before and after they participated in a 10-week conditioning pro-gram confirmed that regular vigorous exercise improves the ability to dissolve blood clots.

Caution: If you already have retinopathy, this may be another story and vigorous exercise may not be wise. See Chapter 11.

A Balancing Act

Diabetes control is always a balancing act between intake (food), which must contain enough glucose to fuel the body, and outgo (bodily functions and exercise, perhaps aided by insulin or oral agents). Your doctor always tries to determine how active you are before deciding on the amount of medication you must take. If you don't exercise, you'll need less food and/or more medication than some-one in exactly the same medical situation who exercises.

To make this balancing act work (and to keep life sim-ple) it is always best to get approximately the same amount of exercise every day; this way you will know just how much medication you need to take, as well as what to eat. Otherwise, you must make constant adjustments.

But if you are a working person, you probably sit at a desk most of the week and do your exercise on weekends, or maybe you only get out to run or bike or walk every few days. In this case, you have to plan ahead, one day at a time. Some people have two different diets, one for sedentary days, another for active days. If they take insulin, they sometimes inject different amounts as well. Unless you are spilling a lot of sugar (never a good idea), you always run the risk if you take insulin of an insulin reaction when you exercise. This is the number one concern of diabetic athletes.

If you don't take insulin, life is obviously a whole lot easier. First, you don't have to be so careful about eating on time. Second, after you have burned up your sugar you will have less extraneous insulin in your bloodstream to cause a reaction. Even if you take oral medication, reactions won't be a problem for you. Oral medication is not oral insulin, and it is extremely rare for people not on insulin to have insulin shock unless they are very ill and debilitated, or haven't eaten at all for a long period of time.

Avoiding Reactions

Let's face it, if you take insulin and your diabetes is in good control—which should always be your goal—you may have to experience an occasional insulin reaction. This is preferable to constant high blood sugar, which will eventually take its toll on your body. See Chapter 11. Ideally, you are taking enough insulin to cover your food and your activities and keep your sugar level normal. When you exercise more than usual, you burn off extra glucose and may become hypoglycemic unless you take precautionary measures.

On a day when you are going to exercise heavily, you

must plan ahead. Either take less insulin or eat more food, or both. This is something you must work out with your own doctor, because everyone's requirements are different; usually an insulin reduction of about 20 percent works out satisfactorily if it is combined with an increase in protein and carbohydrate. Don't every try to make adjustments without your doctor's advice as well as constant urine-testing or finger-stick blood tests to be sure you are not going from one blood-sugar extreme to the other.

Let's take an example. You plan to run this morning. You test your urine or blood and it is negative.

If you take Regular and Intermediate-acting insulin in combination, reduce your Regular dose by 20 percent (if your doctor agrees), or if it is a small dose omit the Regular insulin and at breakfast eat 10 to 20 *extra* grams of carbohydrate *plus* some protein that will slowly convert to carbohydrate in a few hours.

If you take only Intermediate insulin, cut back a few units and increase your food.

When you decide to do your heavy physical activity in the afternoon, remember that Intermediate-acting insulin peaks around 3 P.M. You probably should reduce your Intermediate dose that morning by 20 percent or by whatever amount you and your doctor have decided works best for you.

Some Alternative Arrangements

• For some people a more workable plan is to take the usual dose of insulin, then to add more food to make up the difference, especially when activities aren't predictable in advance.

• For overweight diabetics, lowering the insulin intake is probably better than adding calories. This way, you can lose weight at the same time.

• Now, suppose you plan to exercise today and when testing your urine (always the *second* specimen of the morning) you find that it shows high sugar (3 or 4+). In this case, you can use the exercise to help your insulin bring down the sugar. Take your normal dose and eat a little less carbohydrate at the meal before you start off.

• If, on the other hand, you are going to be exercising *really* rigorously, the recommendation is to take your full complement of food and assume the exercise itself will act like extra insulin.

• Exception: if you wake up with diabetic acidosis, exercise will aggravate your situation. Call off your plans. That's easy, because you won't feel like going through with them anyway.

Snacking for Safety

A carbohydrate or protein-and-carbohydrate snack about a half hour before the run or the game is recommended if your blood sugar is normal or negative. Again, you must work this out with your doctor or by trial and error.

Sometimes planning ahead isn't enough. Perhaps you'll need some quick-acting carbohydrate *during* your exercise. If the tennis match goes into the fourth or fifth set and you still haven't won, your breakfast or lunch plus a snack may not be enough to get you through. Stop for a few seconds, take out some of your emergency rations, which you must *always* carry with you, and have a snack to boost your blood sugar.

For most people, a small amount of carbohydrate about every 20 minutes during very hard exercise is sufficient. You'll soon get a sense of how much you need, and how often. A pitcher for the old Boston Braves had it all worked out in peanuts. If he had to throw more pitches or give up more hits than he'd anticipated, he ate extra peanuts based on the number of balls thrown at the plate.

Along with carbohydrate to counteract low blood sugar, you must also replace lost fluids. Your body needs the fluid you have lost through sweating. Drink plenty of water. If you want to drink one of the commercial electrolyte glucose drinks, keep in mind they are too concentrated for you and may interfere with the rate at which sugar gets into your bloodstream. If it is the only drink available, always dilute it with a lot of water.

Don't wait for a warning that an insulin reaction is coming; sometimes there is none. Anticipate. If you're a newcomer to diabetes or exercise, remember you will soon be able to tell when it is time for a booster. Suppose you are playing baseball. Instead of striking out and sitting down on the bench in your usual fashion, you make a three-base hit. Now you've got to make a mad sprint around the bases. Or you're late for a 5:45 and run a few blocks to catch the train. You haven't planned on it and so you have not adjusted your food or your medication. Now is the time to pull out those emergency rations from your pocket and eat them.

Just a *small* amount of food will do the job. If you need more in 15 minutes, take a little more. (See Chapter 9). Many people panic and overshoot the mark, taking too much sugar to ward off a reaction. While they may have made the train or won the tennis game, now they have to pay the price of very high sugar which may be harder to cope with than the other extreme.

It's best to exercise *after* a meal, though obviously you should give yourself time to do a little digesting first. After you have eaten, your blood-sugar level is on the rise. Before a meal, it may be very low. For most people who take insulin, the best time to exercise is in the morning after breakfast. But if you can only work it out in midafternoon, remember that your longer-acting insulin is peaking at that moment. Besides considering lowering your morning dose, be sure to have a snack first and be on the lookout for reactions.

A Quick Trip to the Bathroom

When you are on insulin, it's essential to test your urine or your blood before going out to do heavy exercise. If it tests negative before you even begin, you will know you need some carbohydrate for sure. In the morning, always test your *second* specimen of urine. That's because your bladder tells you only what has gone on since the last time you urinated. So your first specimen on waking up could either represent a two-hour collection (if you got up to go to the bathroom toward morning), or an 8- or 10-hour collection (if you didn't). The second voiding gives you a clearer reflection of what is happening in your bloodstream at *this* moment. Or use the finger-stick blood-sugar test for an up-to-the-minute report. See Chapter 8.

The Importance of Shaping Up

When you first start an exercise program, don't leap right in and go at it strenuously. Work up to it slowly, after a discussion with your doctor (yes, yes, yes, talk to your doctor even about this). There's probably no reason you can't participate in any kind of sports or exercise like anyone else, but you must give yourself time to adjust your food and medication requirements and to get your body in condition. Sudden strenuous exercise is dangerous for anyone, diabetic or not.

Exercise May Not Be Your Bag

Though everyone needs a certain amount of physical activity to burn calories and sugar, vigorous exercise is not recommended for some diabetics. That's why it is always imperative to consult your physician before you set out to be an athlete. If your diabetes is in poor control, you may do yourself more harm than good. Studies have shown that, rather than lowering blood glucose as in well-controlled people, prolonged strenuous exercise may raise your sugar level as well as increase the production of ketones. So it may actually aggravate your diabetes.

Exercise may also be contraindicated for you if you have certain diabetic complications. Obviously, foot or leg problems may be one of these (again this is individual—sometimes exercise is very helpful in promoting circulation in these areas). Others may include, for example, retinopathy, because rising blood pressure during exercise may cause hemorrhaging; kidney disease because exercise increases albumin excretion; heart disease because of the danger of overexerting (exercise may be just what you need, however, but only under medical supervision and with a program tailor-made for you).

Choosing the Right Injection Site

One simple way to help avoid hypoglycemia (insulin reaction) when you exercise has recently been revealed by a team of Yale University researchers who found that *where* you inject yourself can make all the difference. If you will be using your legs—running, biking—then you should not inject your insulin in a leg that day because it will be absorbed more rapidly, perhaps precipitating a reaction. If you will be using your right arm, choose your left for your injection today. Remember, too, that injections in the arms or abdomen—if these are not your customary sites—can also absorb much more quickly than those in the legs. So you may have to reduce your dose by a few units, unless your sugar is high, if you make a switch to these new areas.

As a general rule, however, it is best to take your shots in one area, such as the thighs, when you won't be exercising strenuously, because the results will tend to be more uniform.

Beware the "Monday Syndrome"

After some really heavy exercise, your insulin requirements may remain at a lower level the following day while your muscles replenish their supplies of glucose and your liver stocks up on glycogen again. You may need to eat more (or take less insulin) to compensate for this. Again, individual judgment is required here because it is true for some diabetics and not others.

Keep a Weather Watch

Your food and insulin needs may also be affected by heat or cold, either of which can make you burn more energy and therefore become more susceptible to a reaction.

Get a Buddy

It is never smart to be alone when you are doing the kind of exercise that may produce a reaction. Activities such as skiing, running, swimming or sailing can be dangerous if no one is around when you need help. Anyway, they are more fun when you have company, so find yourself a fellow athlete. Let that person know you have diabetes and explain what to do if you have a reaction (see Chapter 9).

Check Out Your Wardrobe

The right gear is important for any sport or exercise, but when you are a diabetic you especially want to avoid certain things—overheating, sore feet, sunburn. Wear the proper shoes for your sport, making sure they fit well, do not rub and are well cushioned. Under them, wear absorbent heavy-duty socks that fit smoothly. No lumps. No holes. Check your feet every night for blisters or other injuries. Don't exercise with feet that look like trouble. Watch all of this because diabetics are particularly susceptible to potentially serious circulatory problems. See Chapter 11. Wear layers of clothes so you can shed some if you need to.

Danger: Frostbite

When participating in winter sports, remember to take special care of your hands and feet. If you have poor circulation, this can be vitally important—frostbite is not what you need. Wear a warm hat, lined gloves, wool socks and warm boots. Go inside frequently and check your fingers and toes (as well as your face and ears) to be sure there is no change in color or sensation. Frostbite means a quick trip to the doctor. Don't try to deal with it yourself. If a doctor isn't immediately available, however, immerse the frostbitten area in lukewarm (never hot) water or cover it with a clean cloth or blanket until you see the doctor.

Remember Your Supplies

Be sure whatever you are wearing has pockets, because you will need a place to stash concentrated quick-acting sugar or a small carbohydrate snack, along with your identification card. Some people like to wear a belt designed to hold sugar or candy, the card and even a small plastic bottle for a drink. Others hang a plastic pouch of supplies on their belts. Of course, if you are going to be in one place, such as a tennis court, you can carry your goodies in a separate bag.

No Alcoholic Celebrations

Many people feel that a nip of wine, a shot of whiskey, or a few beers on the ski slopes or at the finish of a tough bout on the playing field is only what they deserve. But athletics and alcohol don't mix, especially for diabetics. Exercise lowers your blood sugar. At the same time, alcohol inhibits the release of glucose from the liver in response to that low blood sugar, and so it may have quite a different effect than you expect. Right now, you need the glucose from your liver to fuel your brain and replenish your supply. If you drink, you may have an insulin reaction then and there. Give up the nip for a little protein or carbohydrate.

Counting the Calories

If you know how much energy you expend for exercise, you can prepare for it in food or medication. Take a look at this chart, which indicates how many calories each activity is worth. As we have said, one calorie is the amount of energy required for a seated man to turn a doorknob.

CALORIE USAGE TABLE*
(per hour)

Bicycling (5½ mph)	270
Cycling (13 mph)	670
Hill Climbing (slope 1 in 5.7, with 5 kg. load)	640
Roller/Ice Skating	350
Running (6 mph)	630
Running (10 mph)	900
Skiing (10 mph)	600
Snowshoeing (soft snow, 4 km/hr)	830
Squash and Handball	610
Swimming (crawl, 45 yd per minute)	690
Table Tennis	360
Tennis	430
Walking (2½ mph)	220
Walking (3½ mph)	290
Wood Chopping	420

* Passmore, R. and J.U.G.A. Durnin, "Human Energy Expenditure." *Journal of Physiology* (Cambridge University Press, 1955), 35:801—839, as quoted in *Diabetes Forecast*, January–February 1981. © American Diabetes Association. Reprinted with permission.

SIX

Taking Oral Agents

Swallowing a couple of small pills every day is much more appealing and less complicated than giving yourself insulin injections. So if the oral hypoglycemic drugs work for you, consider yourself lucky. There is little need to worry about reactions, no concern about always eating on time, no fuss and muss with needles and syringes and measuring out insulin.

The oral hypoglycemic agents are not for every diabetic because they require that your pancreas has functioning islet cells capable of secreting insulin. Juvenile-type diabetics cannot benefit from them. The typical person for whom oral agents work well is a "mild" diabetic who would probably require less than 40 units of insulin, and was diagnosed after the age of 40 or 50.

The oral agents are not oral insulin. They are not even related to insulin. Instead, they are synthetic drugs that lower your blood sugar. One theory is that they stimulate your pancreas to recognize that the glucose level of your blood has risen and to release the appropriate insulin in response. Another explains the agents' ability to lower blood sugar as an increased response by the liver to metabolize glucose more efficiently, turning sugar into glycogen to be stored or burned as fuel.

The drugs commonly used today are the sulfonylureas (Orinase, Dymelor, Tolinase, Diabinese, Diabeta, Micronase, and Glucotrol). These were discovered by a French scientist who was looking for an effective antibiotic and found that a type of sulfa drug had the secondary effect of lowering blood sugar. The drugs are also thought to perform an additional function: to increase the number and efficiency of the insulin receptors on muscle and fat cells, thereby allowing insulin to enter the cells and help them metabolize sugar. Think of insulin as a key and each receptor as a door. By increasing the number of doors, assuming you have enough keys, more glucose can penetrate the cell walls.

Are Oral Agents Dangerous?

In the opinion of most diabetologists today, oral hypoglycemic agents do *not* increase your chances of heart attack.

More than 10 years ago, an extensive eight-year study called the University Group Diabetes Program linked the oral hypoglycemic agents with an increased risk of death from heart disease. The study's conclusions caused many doctors to stop prescribing the pills and replace them with insulin injections if their patients' diabetes could not be controlled with diet.

These conclusions have now been challenged by many diabetologists, and both the American Diabetic Association and the American Medical Association have stated there is not enough data to justify them. The ADA said that some inferences of the report deserved "restudy and modification." Questions have been raised about the methods of choosing patients for the research, the treatment and the way the data was interpreted.

Doctors who have been prescribing the oral hypoglycemics for over 20 years have found no increase in heart disease among their patients. Nor have other studies (including one at Boston's Joslin Clinic, the most famous diabetic clinic in the world, that compared 500 diabetics on oral agents with 500 matched diabetics on insulin) found any differences in the incidence of heart attacks.

So most doctors today are once again recommending the oral hypoglycemics for appropriate patients, because these drugs present far fewer problems than insulin injections do.

My opinion can be summed up this way: If I were a diabetic who was unable to control my diabetes with diet alone, and could achieve a normal blood-sugar level without having to take a shot every day and without having to be concerned with insulin reactions and rigid eating schedules, I would certainly choose the pills. And, based on evidence today, I would not worry about a heart attack.

Kinds of Oral Agents

There are seven varieties of sulfonylureas available in the United States today. From the weakest to the strongest, they are:

Orinase, the first successful sulfonylurea compound on the American market and the most commonly used today. The least powerful of the drugs, it is sold in 500 mg tablets. You may require only one tablet, or up to six a day given in divided doses.

Dymelor, slightly stronger, has a secondary effect of lowering the level of uric acid, which is high in many diabetics and could lead to kidney stones. Available in 250 and 500 mg tablets, it is given in single or divided doses up to 1500 mg a day.

Tolinase, available in 100, 250 and 500 mg tablets, is also prescribed up to 1000 mg a day. An advantage of this drug is its diuretic effect. Some diabetics tend to retain fluid and so this form of oral agent may be best for them.

Diabinese, the strongest of the four original oral agents, is made in 100 and 250 mg tablets and since the drug remains in the body for about 36 hours, the dose is never split but always taken at one time—before breakfast. Diabinese produces an "Antabuse effect" in some people when they consume alcohol. If this happens in your case, you will quickly develop a beet-red facial flush, a choking sensation and perhaps a headache. This can happen even when you eat food that has been cooked in wine or liquor so you must always inquire about dishes served away from home before taking a bite. While this is a nuisance, there may be reason to consider yourself fortunate if you suffer from the Antabuse effect. Recent research shows that the diabetic who has such reactions runs a lesser risk of succumbing to retinopathy and other major cardiovascular diseases.

Diabeta, Micronase (both glyburides), and *Glucotrol* (glipizide), the new sulfonylureas, are the strongest and most effective oral agents today. They are all mildly diuretic. Diabeta and Micronase come in 1.25, 2.5 and 5 mg tablets and are prescribed up to 20 mg a day, taken in one dose before breakfast. Glucotrol is available in 5 and 10 mg tablets and may be taken twice a day because its effects don't last as long. It is prescribed up to 20 mg or more a day.

Another kind of oral agent, popular for many years, has been banned except in special cases by the U.S. Food and Drug Administration. DBI (or Phenformin) is a biguanide rather than a sulfonylurea preparation and belongs to a different family of compounds. It was taken off the market because it was believed to be responsible for deaths due to lactic acidosis among diabetics with renal and liver disease. However, doctors may obtain this drug for certain patients through the offices of the FDA. It is prescribed in combination with other oral agents for people who cannot, or will not, take the insulin they require. These include blind people who cannot see the numbers on the insulin syringe, others who cannot manipulate the syringe because of arthritic hands and a few who simply refuse to take injections. Together with Tolinase, for example, DBI can effect good and safe control if it is used with caution.

ORAL HYPOGLYCEMIC AGENTS

Trade name	Generic name	Size	Usual Daily Dosage
Orinase	Tolbutamide	500 mg	500 to 3000 mg
Dymelor	Acetohexamide	250 mg and 500 mg	250 to 1500 mg
Tolinase	Tolazamide	100 mg, 250 mg and 500 mg	100 to 1000 mg
Diabinese	Chlorpropamide	100 mg and 250 mg	100 to 500 mg
DiaBeta	Glyburide	1.25 mg, 2.5 mg and 5 mg	1.25 to 10 mg
Micronase	Glyburide	1.25 mg, 2.5 mg and 5 mg	1.25 to 10 mg
Glucotrol	Glipizide	5 mg and 10 mg	5 to 10 mg
DBI	Phenformin	25 mg	25 to 100 mg

Diet Is Still Important

Just because you are taking oral agents instead of insulin does not mean that you are home free. You still cannot eat whatever you like. Hot fudge sundaes are still not an option, nor is too much food of any kind. For any diabetic, diet is the most important part of the therapy. The pills will not transform you into a normal person with a normal pancreas that turns out as much insulin as you need to respond to an overload of sugar.

If you eat too much, you—like an insulin-dependent diabetic—may end up in the hospital in a coma. Not only that, but if your diabetes is consistently out of control, even to a degree that isn't obvious to you, you are greatly increasing your risk of developing diabetic complications in the future. Just like an insulin-dependent person, you are a real diabetic. However, if you maintain your proper weight, eat sensibly, and get enough exercise, it is possible you may no longer need the oral agents and will not be considered diabetic but merely someone with a tendency toward the disease.

Extra pills are not like extra insulin. Many people think, if they overdose on food, they can compensate by taking extra pills. They cannot. They will simply go out of control and have high blood sugar, which is just as harmful to them as to any other diabetic. When your fixed maximum effect has been reached, additional pills will do no good.

Tally Your Tests

You must also test your blood or urine regularly. If you are well controlled, make tests twice a day—before breakfast and before bed or before supper. If you are not, do it three or four times daily until your sugar is down. Keep a record of the results and take this to your doctor. Together you can decide how to change your diet and/or your activities so you may not have to switch to insulin.

Illnesses, excessive sugar in your diet, less exercise, more stress, etc., can cause you to spill sugar and perhaps acetone. If your sugar is high, always test for acetone. If acetone is present, confer with your doctor. A temporary supplement of insulin may be what you need. Going over to insulin during an illness or pregnancy does not make you insulin-dependent. When you no longer need the shots, you can probably return to your former regime.

When You Are Sick

Whenever you have an infection, especially when it is accompanied by a fever, your insulin requirements will rise as your liver releases extra glucose as part of the body's defenses against attack and as more glucose is formed from protein when you are under stress. But you may not get enough insulin response from your pill-primed pancreas to handle this increased sugar. If your tests show prolonged high sugars, something must be done to avoid acidosis.

Your doctor will probably suggest, if you normally take only a small amount of oral medication, that you be very strict about your diet and perhaps raise your dosage to increase the pills' efficiency. When you are already taking your maximum effective dose, however, taking more is not the answer. You have reached your limit of insulin production.

If your blood sugar does not return to normal, you'll need to turn to insulin temporarily, alone or as a supplement. Unless you are an old hand at this, do nothing on your own. Let your doctor make the decisions. Probably 5 to 10 units of Regular insulin every two hours will turn the tide.

That is why you must know how to give yourself injections and keep a bottle of Regular insulin stored in your refrigerator. (Replace it when it becomes outdated.) Your doctor will tell you how often to take it.

Temporary insulin injections will also be needed by most diabetics on oral agents when they have major surgery. The reason is the same—increased need for insulin during stress.

Possible Side Effects of the Oral Agents

Once in a while, a diabetic reacts unfavorably to the oral hypoglycemic agents. The usual side effects include nausea and other gastointestinal problems, fever, skin rashes, itching. If these symptoms do not diminish and then disappear at your lowest possible dosage, the only solution is to stop taking the pills and switch over to insulin or to be stricter with your diet.

Are Reactions a Concern?

Hypoglycemic reactions are an *extremely* rare occurrence when you take oral agents because your pancreas is sensitized to respond only to the glucose content of your bloodstream. The insulin does not pour out as soon as you swallow your pills, as it does from an injection, but waits until it is required.

But, under very special circumstances, reactions are possible. Too high a dosage, unexpected and very heavy exercise, consistent insufficiency of food (especially among the elderly, who may not have a sufficient store of glycogen), can all trigger a hypoglycemic reaction. Usually the reaction is mild and easily reversible because your blood sugar does not drop as far or as fast as it would if you were taking insulin. It may make you feel weak, trembly, faint or headachy.

A much more severe reaction can occur, however, and may be quite prolonged. This is usually the result of the overlapping effects of long-acting oral agents.

But sometimes it happens for other reasons. Liver or kidney disease, for example, can affect the behavior of the oral agents. And so can the interaction of other drugs that are detoxified in the liver. These include:

Coumadin (an anticoagulant)
Butazolidine (an antiinflammatory)
Sulfonamides (antibiotics)
Benemid (for gout)

Dilantin (for epilepsy)
Atromid S or Clofibrate (for high cholesterol)
Mood ameliorators such as MAO inhibitors

The treatment for hypoglycemia is always the same—eat some quickly absorbed carbohydrate, along with some protein. Because the hypoglycemia may not be reversed quickly if it is due to overlapping oral-agent doses or disease, your blood sugar should be closely monitored until you're back to normal.

Be *sure* to inform any doctor who treats you that you are diabetic and take oral agents, so that this will be taken into account if other drugs are prescribed.

Never skip your meals or snacks, and remember to eat extra food if you are going to engage in heavy exercise.

Tell your doctor if you ever have reactions. Because reactions are so rare when you take oral agents, the reason must be discovered.

Other Drug Interactions

Inderal, a drug prescribed for hypertension, can block the secretion of insulin and cause the oral agent to be ineffective in some cases.

And the effects of most barbiturates, sedatives and hypnotics can be seriously prolonged when you take sulfonyurea agents.

Will the Pills Ever Become Ineffective?

For most people, the oral agents continue to do their job indefinitely. Though it was once thought that their effect always diminishes after five or ten years, it has been found that only 17 percent of pill-takers have "secondary failure" and so must start taking insulin instead.

If your diabetes control seems to be worse, the most likely explanation is that you aren't paying attention to your diet or your need for exercise. Neither pills nor insulin shots will keep you from all the problems of diabetes without proper living habits. But if you are in the minority whose internal insulin production does diminish with time, a stronger or longer-acting oral agent may help reestablish your control. If not, then you must turn to insulin.

If You Forget to Take Your Dose

It is not a good idea to omit your dose of oral agent, but it isn't a serious matter if you skip it only once in a while. That is because you do make some insulin on your own, and a brief period without the agent won't raise your blood sugar to dangerous levels. Simply take your pill when you remember it. If you have gone as long as a whole day without the medication and your urine tests show high sugar, be sure to take your pill now. If you are very symptomatic (excessive thirst or urination), call your doctor promptly because you may be heading for acidosis.

SEVEN

Going the Insulin Route

ALL IDDMs (juvenile-onset diabetics) and those NIDDMs (maturity-onset diabetics) whose blood sugar cannot be controlled by diet therapy or oral agents must go the insulin route. This means daily injections, a prospect nobody regards with great joy. But once you accept them as essential to your health, they can be managed without turning your life upside down. Eating on time, sticking to your diet, testing your urine, adjusting your dose, being alert to low blood sugar as well as high can all become routine parts of your daily existence that need not always dominate your thoughts. If insulin therapy is new to you, this may be hard to believe, but with time and experience you can learn to go about your business despite being an insulin-dependent diabetic.

Consider a diabetic's fate before this miracle drug was discovered: Before 1922, adults who developed diabetes were lucky to live another 10 years, youngsters a few months. Diet was the only known treatment and starving was the alternative to diabetic coma.

In 1921, Drs. Charles Best and Frederick Banting extracted a substance from a steer's pancreas and injected it into a diabetic dog, promptly lowering the dog's blood sugar. With that success, the outlook for diabetics changed overnight. Drs. Best and Banting next gave the new extract to each other, waited 24 hours, then injected it into a twelve-year-old diabetic boy who was near death but made a dramatic recovery on a steady regime of insulin injections. In only a year, Best and Banting and other scientists developed the techniques for mass-producing the miracle hormone, literally creating life for people who previously had been doomed.

Today's Insulin

The insulin used today—if not synthesized from bacteria—is still extracted from pigs and cattle, but it has changed radically from the liquid that filled that first syringe. It has been made more pure until today, with the new monocomponent insulins, most contaminants such as proinsulin and glucagon have been removed, making them much less likely to cause allergic reactions and perhaps some of the common diabetic complications as well.

Today's insulins are combined with other substances that modify the rate at which they are absorbed, so they may be prescribed according to individual needs. The solubility of insulin, which determines how quickly it enters the bloodstream and goes into action, is decided by three factors: the physical form (amorphous or crystalline) and, if crystalline, the size of the crystals; the amount of zinc salts added; and the nature of the buffer solution holding it.

Some of the most exciting news involves the development of synthetic insulin that, unlike the animal varieties, is biologically identical to human insulin. Made by bacteria that have been genetically altered by "gene-splicing" techniques, it does an excellent job. One thing is sure: now that we know it works well, there will always be plenty of insulin. Some manufacturers predict a shortage of animal pancreases in 10 to 20 years. If you use human insulin, keep in mind that it may act faster and may not last as long as the other insulins, so you may need more shots a day.

Kinds of Insulin

Many varieties and strengths of insulin are now on the market, and only your doctor can prescribe which one or combination you should take and in what amounts. Everyone's needs are different and much trial and error are usually required before you find your proper track.

Insulins vary in several ways: how long they take to start lowering your blood sugar; how long this lowering ability lasts; when they "peak" or provide their maximum effect; and their strength.

Fast-acting: *Regular* insulin (clear) goes into effect very quickly, in less than an hour, and peaks in 2 to 3 hours. Though it lasts a couple of hours longer than that in the bloodstream, its effectiveness diminishes rapidly. In an emergency, Regular insulin can be given intravenously for even faster action.

Semilente is another insulin that wastes little time going into action. It works within 1 hour after injection, peaks in 5 to 7 hours, and can be found in the bloodstream for 12 to 16 hours.

Intermediate-acting: *NPH* and *Lente* insulins are both in the intermediate group and are the most frequently prescribed of all. They last about 24 hours, start to work about 1 to 1½ hours after injection, and peak in 8 to 12 hours. This means they have a small amount of action before lunch and have their major effect in midafternoon.

Long-acting: *Ultralente* and *PZI* (protamine zinc insulin) do not start working effectively for 4 to 8 hours, peak 14 to 20 hours after the injection, and last 24 to 36 hours in the bloodstream.

Fast-acting insulins are rarely used alone on a daily basis, unless you are on a multiple-injection plan which means you inject yourself several times a day with small amounts of insulin in response to your blood-sugar level. These insulins are usually combined with intermediate forms for daily use, or used only when you need insulin in a hurry.

The intermediates are prescribed by most diabetologists today because they cover you with insulin 24 hours a day, including your three meals and the glucose released from your liver during the night.

The long-acting insulins are not prescribed by many doctors today, except in special cases, because their prolonged duration in the body can vary and precipitate severe hypoglycemic reactions, especially in the early morning hours before you wake up.

GUIDE TO INSULIN

Type	Onset of Action	Peak Action	Duration
Regular	Less than 1 hour	2–3 hours	5–8 hours
Velosulin	Less than 1 hour	2–3 hours	5–8 hours
Humulin	Less than 1 hour	2–3 hours	5–8 hours
Actrapid	Less than 1 hour	2–3 hours	5–8 hours
Actrapid-Human	Less than 1 hour	2–3 hours	5–8 hours
Semilente	Less than 1 hour	5–7 hours	12–16 hours
NPH	1–1½ hours	8–12 hours	24 hours
NPH Iletin II	1–1½ hours	8–12 hours	24 hours
Lente	1–1½ hours	8–12 hours	24 hours
Monotard	2½ hours	8–12 hours	24 hours
Monotard-Human	2 hours	8–12 hours	under 24 hours
Humulin-N	2 hours	8–12 hours	under 24 hours
Lentard	2½ hours	8–12 hours	24 hours

Insulatard	2½ hours	8–12 hours	24 hours
Mixtard	2½ hours	8–12 hours	24 hours
Ultralente	4–5 hours	14–20 hours	24–36 hours or more
PZI	4–8 hours	14–20 hours	36 hours
Ultratard	5 hours	10 to 30 hours	36 hours or more
PZI Iletin II	4–8 hours	14–20 hours	24–36 hours or more

Insulin Strengths

Today, in the United States, insulin is almost always prescribed in U-100 strength. This means there are 100 units of insulin per cubic centimeter (cc) of fluid. Until recently, insulin was also available in strengths of U-40 and U-80, or 40 and 80 units of insulin per cc of fluid. This was confusing to many people and mistakes in dosage were frequently made when switching from one strength to another. On the recommendation of the American Diabetes Association and other medical experts, the two lower strengths are being phased out of production in this country and virtually all doctors have stopped prescribing them.

In the meantime, remember: *a unit of insulin is always the same,* no matter what strength you use. In the early days, a unit was the amount of insulin that would lower the blood sugar of a four-pound rabbit to 45 mgs percent. Today the unit is standardized all over the world. If you are in another country where you may be able to buy only U-40 or U-80, you can still use it, but you must know how to translate from one strength to the other.

A unit of one strength is interchangeable with a unit of any other. It has the same potency and blood-sugar lowering effect. What differs is the amount of solution or liquid in which the insulin is held. One cc of U-40 insulin contains 40 units of insulin. One cc of U-80 contains 80 units.

One cc of U-100 contains 100 units of insulin. Therefore, one unit of U-40 is larger *in volume* (because of the water content) than a unit of U-80 or U-100, but the strength of one unit is always the same.

So, *one unit is one unit,* and can be exchanged for one unit of a different strength. BUT you must use a syringe that corresponds with your insulin (i.e., a U-100 syringe for U-100 insulin—both have orange caps) in order to avoid errors.

In an Emergency

If you *must* use a syringe that does not correspond to your insulin, then you can make the translation. For example, if you run out of U-100 insulin, and must use U-40 (only U-40 is available in some countries) with a U-100 syringe: multiply your usual *volume* (not your units) of U-100 by 2½. This will give you an equivalent U-40 dose. In other words, you need a larger *volume* (2½ times as much) of U-40 to equal the same number of units of U-100 because it is less concentrated.

10 units on U-100 syringe	= 4 units of U-40 insulin
20	= 8 units
30	= 12 units
40	= 16 units
50	= 20 units
Etc.	

Syringe Strategy

Insulin syringes come in many sizes and shapes and it doesn't matter too much which one you use as long as you are always certain you use one that corresponds with your insulin strength. Syringes are marked U-40, U-80 and U-100, and they are color-coded to match the insulin bottles as well. U-100 syringes are available in 50-unit sizes for people who take very small doses. Each line is 1 unit rather than 2 units as in the 100-unit size.

Today most diabetics in this country needn't be concerned about matching syringes to insulin because most doctors are prescribing only U-100 and the other strengths will soon be unavailable.

Most people today use disposable syringes and needles that are made of plastic. These can be used a few times (as long as the needles are sharp) without too much concern about sterility. Consult your doctor about this. Other people choose the reusable syringes and needles that are kept in alcohol and boiled once a week to sterilize them. The syringes can be used indefinitely. The needles may be sharpened and will last for months.

The thinnest ½-inch needles—25, 26, 27 or 28 gauge—cause the least discomfort and are the most popular. Needles that are thinner than 25 gauge tend to clog or break. Needles that are thicker may hurt! If you are heavy, you may need a ⅝-inch needle instead of the ½-inch length.

Some timid people prefer to use automatic injectors, available in any drugstore, because they find it too traumatic to stick needles in themselves. But today's needles are so sharp that the prick is hardly noticeable. Besides, the automatic injectors must be kept sterile, washed and boiled. Most diabetics agree that the disposable syringes are the handiest and easiest to use, though they cost more money.

Allergic Reactions to Insulin

One problem many insulin-dependent diabetics have always had is an allergic response at the site of the injection, especially when they have just started to take insulin or when they take it only occasionally. Often it occurs six or

more weeks after starting to take injections. The symptoms
—redness, swelling, itchiness—are usually mild and local-
ized and completely gone in a couple of weeks.

Allergic reactions have become almost a problem of the
past because they are seldom caused by newer monocomponent insulins, especially purified pork insulin,
which is the closet to human insulin, and are even less
frequent with human insulin that is made by gene-splicing.
It may make us feel less than gods to realize that the 51
amino acids of pig insulin differ only by one amino acid
from the human. The cow, on the other hand, is three
amino acids, plus some hoofs and a tail, away. The human
insulins, made by neither pigs nor cows but bacteria, show
no biological difference at all though occasional allergic
reactions have been reported.

In the meantime, sometimes a diabetic must be desensi-
tized to insulin by taking very small doses four or more
times a day, increasing the amount very slowly until the
proper dose is reached with no skin reactions. Doctors occasionally prescribe a tiny amount of antihistamine or cortisone mixed by injection into the insulin vial by the phar-
macist to counteract the allergic response.

Insulin Resistance

Though these allergic diabetics are very sensitive to insulin, others are very resistant to it, requiring vast amounts
before it begins to do its job of lowering sugar effectively.
If you need more than 200 units a day, you are considered
to be insulin-resistant. Sometimes the answer is cortisone
therapy or a switch in insulins.

Insulin resistance is the result of a buildup of antibodies
in response to the insulin, producing an allergy. Then
other antibodies form to block the first ones. If too much
of the second group is formed, it will interfere with the ac-

tion of the insulin you take, making it much less effective, and you will need considerably larger doses.

The resistance may last for months or years. When it vanishes, it may do so very suddenly, so suddenly that all that insulin you are taking can give you a tremendous insulin shock. Be aware this can happen and always be sure to carry emergency sweets wherever you go, as well as a glucagon injection kit.

How to Give Yourself an Injection

Though it seems very simple to an experienced person, injecting yourself is frightening for the beginner until you get the hang of it. Many people practice on something other than themselves—an orange, for example—until they have perfected a smooth technique. Even if you don't take insulin but control your diabetes with diet or oral agents, you must know how to inject it because a time may come—during an illness, perhaps—when you may require it temporarily.

GETTING READY: THE MATERIALS YOU NEED

Here's what you will need at hand:

1. Insulin

2. A syringe that corresponds to the strength of your insulin. This may be a disposable syringe with a disposable needle, in which case you merely unwrap it, use it and throw it away (or use it a few times before throwing it away). If it is a reusable syringe, you must have a container filled with alcohol where you will store it between injections, and a small pot in which you will boil it once a week. Always be sure you have at least *two* syringes and needles on hand.

3. Alcohol (70 percent ethyl/91 percent isopropyl).

4. Absorbent cotton or prepackaged alcohol swabs.

FILLING THE SYRINGE WITH INSULIN

1. Remember to keep the needle sterile. Don't touch it with your fingers or anything else. With a reusable syringe, squirt out any water or alcohol remaining in the syringe. This is obviously unnecessary with an unused disposable syringe.

2. Shake the insulin bottle gently, inverting it to make sure it is thoroughly mixed.

3. Wipe off the rubber stopper on the top of the bottle with a piece of alcohol-soaked cotton. Do not remove the stopper from the bottle.

4. Draw the plunger back to the mark on the syringe that corresponds with your dose of insulin. This fills the space with air.

5. Insert the needle through the rubber stopper into the bottle. Push the plunger all the way down, pushing the air into the bottle.

6. With the needle in the bottle, turn the bottle upside down and pull the plunger back *just beyond* the mark showing your correct dose.

7. Slowly push the plunger back to the correct mark for your dose. This will expel the air bubbles. Don't worry about a few little bubbles. They won't hurt you. You would require much more air than that to do you in.

8. When the syringe is filled with the correct dose, pull the needle out of the bottle. Don't let the bottle hang upright on the needle because the needle may bend.

MIXING TWO INSULINS IN ONE SYRINGE

Let's suppose your doctor has instructed you to take 4 Regular and 10 Lente units of insulin.

1. Draw air into the syringe up to the 10-unit line.

2. Put the needle through the center of the rubber cap of the Lente (cloudy) bottle and inject the 10 units of air into the bottle.

3. Withdraw the needle, *empty*.

4. Draw 4 units of air into the same syringe.

5. Push the needle through the rubber cap of the Regular bottle (this insulin is clear) and inject this air into the bottle.

6. Withdraw with 4 units of Regular insulin.

7. Turn Lente bottle upside down and insert the same needle into that bottle.

8. Slowly pull the plunger back to total 14 units. You now have 4 units of Regular and 10 units of Lente in your syringe.

CHOOSING THE SPOT

Insulin may be injected into the *fronts* of your thighs (the most commonly chosen site); the *backs* and *sides* of your upper arms; the *front* and *sides* of your abdomen; or the *top* of your buttocks. To be sure to reach muscle tissue rather than bone, major blood vessels or nerves, never inject into the outsides of your thighs, the lower or inner areas of the buttocks, or below the knee. Be careful to stay far away from the radial nerve that is located near your elbow. Because fatty tissue provides the best locations, a really thin person will usually use the thighs or buttocks, while fatter people have more options.

The most important thing to remember is to rotate your sites. Don't inject in spots within one inch of each other in the same month. If you continually use one location, it may become hardened and scarred, or lumps of fat may appear under the skin. This is not beautiful, the needle won't go in very easily and the insulin will not be absorbed as well as it should. This has become much less of a problem, however, since the purer monocompent and human insulins have become widely available. Best to make a chart so you do not return to the exact same spot within a month.

The best method is to rotate around the same anatomi-

cal area, such as the thighs, because insulin absorption var-
ies in different parts of the body. If you don't compensate
for the difference, you may throw your control off. When
you inject in your abdomen, for example, it absorbs, according to a recent study, 86 percent more quickly than in
your leg, and 30 percent more quickly than in your arm.
You will achieve much more consistency in the effectiveness of your insulin without added concern about reactions
or high sugar if you don't jump around from one area of
your body to another.

If you want to inject your abdomen or arm, an area you
probably do not usually use, you may have to reduce your
dose by about 5 units unless your sugar is high and you
want to take advantage of the greater absorption. If you
aren't aware of the differences, you may have some unexpected reactions.

Just to confuse matters, it is important to remember that
insulin absorption also increases if you inject in an area
that is going to get immediate heavy exercise. So, if you are
going to go biking, don't inject in your leg. If you'll be
playing tennis, don't choose your racquet arm. Unless, of
course, you have high sugar and want to bring it down
quickly.

INJECTING THE INSULIN

Wipe the area with a piece of cotton soaked in alcohol, or
a prepared alcohol swab. With one hand, pinch a large
fold of flesh between your thumb and forefinger, at least
three inches apart. Or, to inject into your upper arm, lean
against a door to push your flesh up.

With the other hand, pick up the syringe like a pencil or
a dart. Push the needle quickly and firmly into the skin,
straight in vertical to the skin. Pull back slightly on the
plunger with the needle in place. If blood appears at the
tip of the syringe, you have hit a small blood vessel. This

isn't dangerous but may cause bleeding and bruising. (A recent report found no harm in continuing with the injection rather than withdrawing the needle.) Try to take no longer than about five seconds for the whole job. Now release the pinch and press an alcohol pad next to the needle and pull it out.

If you have used a reusable syringe, take it apart and rinse all of the parts in clean water. Store it in the container with alcohol.

To prevent the possibility of a clogged needle, always inject the insulin *quickly* after pushing in the needle. But if the needle does clog, withdraw it and *write down* the number of units you injected (your original dose minus the number of units remaining in the syringe). Take a new syringe and inject *only* the amount you still need to complete your full dose.

Occasionally you may notice that a little insulin squirts out when you make your injection and you don't know how many units you have lost. Or, as you take the needle out, there is more than the usual flow of blood, and again, you wonder if you have lost insulin. *Never* give yourself another injection. Probably you have not lost much, so simply eat a little less, check your urine or blood before lunch and dinner to see if you are spilling. If your sugar is high, you may need an extra dose (perhaps 4 to 5 units) of Regular insulin. Check with your doctor.

If Your Vision Is Poor

If you can't see the numbers on the syringe, you may be glad to know that you can buy special inexpensive appliances that will enable you to tell with your fingers when you have filled the syringe with the prescribed dose of insulin. Your ADA affiliate or Juvenile Diabetes Foundation chapter will tell you where they may be purchased.

Storing Your Insulin

The new insulins will keep very nicely at room temperature for over a year without losing their potency, so if you don't like to inject cold insulin you needn't refrigerate the bottle in use. But try to keep it in a cool, dim place, and be careful not to subject it to extreme temperatures.

Store your extra bottles in the refrigerator, but *never* put it in the freezer. Freezing destroys the insulin's potency. If a bottle freezes, throw it out. Never let it get very hot either. Don't keep it in your car's glove compartment, or on a window sill in the sun or near the oven.

Insulin is marked with an expiration date. After that date, it may start losing its strength. In an emergency, outdated insulin may be used until you have a new supply. It loses strength very slowly. Under ordinary circumstances, though, if you see yours is outdated, don't use it.

Regular insulin must be clear and colorless, just like water. If it becomes cloudy or discolored, don't use it. The other insulins should not become granular or clumped or form a deposit of solid particles. If they do, do not use them.

Insulin Pumps

A recent invention called an insulin pump can solve serious problems for diabetics who cannot control their sugar any other way. These people may include some juvenile-type diabetics who are exceedingly hard to regulate, some pregnant women and brittle diabetics who swing rapidly from one extreme of blood sugar to the other. Most people can do just as well on their own, but occasionally the pump can completely change an uncontrolled person's life.

The pump is a fairly small device worn on a belt

around the waist. Battery-driven, it is programmed to deliver subcutaneously, by way of a 12- to 40-inch catheter, tiny amounts of insulin at set times around the clock, as well as four larger doses 30 minutes before each meal and the bedtime snack. The pump simulates as closely as possible the natural production of insulin and has been responsible for impressive results for some diabetics who never did well before.

On the other hand, the pump is not without problems. It is awkward. The tubes can get clogged, the mechanism can fail. Best, if you can, to stick to the rules and do without.

In development right now are at least two other kinds of devices designed to deliver insulin automatically. One consists of a sensor that monitors glucose levels continuously, a mini-computer to interpret the sensor's findings, and a pump to infuse insulin in response. However, this "closed loop feedback" device is at present the size of a television set, and therefore is not exactly handy for diabetics who are not in bed. Other research involves using beta cells implanted in the body to function as a pancreatic replacement. See Chapter 17.

Mixed and Split Doses

Most diabetics today take a mixed dose of Regular and Intermediate-acting insulin at the same time, using one injection or more a day. The Regular insulin has a short action span and works quickly. The Intermediate-acting insulin works over a longer period of time.

Many people get along very well with just one injection a day but others do much better with a split dose, taking most of their daily amount (perhaps 75 percent) in the morning and the rest in another injection before dinner or bed. This allows a fairly close approximation of the normal physiological pattern, smoothing out the peaks and valleys of available insulin.

If you tend to have late-morning or afternoon insulin reactions with only one daily injection, your doctor will undoubtedly recommend the split dose, probably combining Regular and Intermediate insulin each time.

Multiple Injections

To get optimum control, even more than two shots a day are required by some people. Obviously, if you can do well without multiple injections you won't want them, because this regime is not easy. But it is well worth the bother if this is the only way you can maintain good control. Your gains are greater than your efforts.

Of course, most insulin-taking diabetics must take multiple injections during stress periods such as an illness or a pregnancy.

Whether you take the multiple injections on a daily basis or only temporarily, your insulin intake must be adjusted according to your test results. If, for example, you are taking a combination of Regular and Intermediate-acting insulin and get these results, you must make these changes:

Before Breakfast	Before Lunch	Before Dinner	Before Bed	Add
Negative	4 +	Negative	Negative	Add more units of Regular insulin.
Negative	4 +	4+	4+	Increase Intermediate insulin (and bedtime snack if you get nighttime reactions).

Before Breakfast	Before Lunch	Before Dinner	Before Bed	Add
Negative	Negative	Negative	4 +	Add Regular insulin before dinner or reduce carbohydrates at dinner.
4 +	Negative	Negative	4 +	Add Regular and Intermediate-acting or Regular alone before dinner.
4 +	Negative	Negative	Negative	Reduce bedtime snack or take small amount of Intermediate insulin at bedtime.

"Oops! I've Made a Mistake!"

It happens to everyone. You forget to take your insulin, you take too much, or get the amounts mixed up. Don't panic. Here is how to deal with your mistakes:

Forgetting to take your insulin: Suppose you get up in the morning, eat your breakfast, go to work or school and suddenly in the middle of the day realize you didn't take your morning shot.

Now you must take more Regular (because you are behind in the insulin you need) and less longer-acting (because there is less time before your next morning shot). Let's suppose you normally take 10 Regular and 30 Intermediate-acting in the morning. If it is now about 11 A.M., take your injection, using slightly less but close to your normal dose. If you don't realize your omission until 3:30 in the afternoon and you start having symptoms of high sugar, take 20 Regular and 20 Intermediate. You need quicker action (therefore the increased Regular) over a shorter time span (therefore the decreased Intermediate).

Suppose you are at work or school or far from home

when you realize you haven't taken your insulin. Call a doctor in the area and arrange to go to the office for a shot. Or go to the emergency room at the local hospital, telling the admitting clerk you cannot sit around waiting but must be attended to quickly. A third possibility is to get the name and telephone number of a drugstore in the area and then ask your own doctor to call this pharmacy and prescribe a syringe and insulin for you.

Taking a double dose: Suppose you take your shot, have your breakfast, and give yourself another shot by mistake. Once in a while this won't hurt you if you eat enough to compensate for it—but don't make a habit of it. Meantime, have a field day. Have all those ice cream sodas, chocolate sundaes, coconut cakes you've been longing for. Space them out during the day and have a good snack before bed. Set your clock for 3 A.M. Get up and have another snack if you are still negative. The next morning, start your usual regime.

Reversing your split doses: A common error is to take what you normally take in the morning (the larger portion of your split dose) in the afternoon before dinner. In other words, suppose you normally take 10 Regular and 30 Intermediate in the morning, and 4 Regular and 10 Intermediate before dinner. Today you take your morning dose and then, before dinner, you unthinkingly take the same dose again, much more than you should at that hour. Again, eating is the answer. Eat more at dinner. Have a large bedtime snack and set your alarm clock for 3 A.M. Get up and check your urine. If it is negative, have some more goodies.

Preparing for an Emergency

Always have a bottle of Regular insulin stored in your refrigerator, even if you don't use it ordinarily. It will keep almost indefinitely though you should replace it when it becomes outdated. Regular insulin is always used when you need quick action.

Insulin in Foreign Countries

Insulin may be purchased all over the world and it is the same as you buy at home, whether or not it is made by an American manufacturer. Just be sure to buy the proper strength, or, if you cannot, also buy a syringe that corresponds to the strength you will be using. See Chapter 16.

Are You a "Brittle" Diabetic?

A brittle diabetic is insulin-dependent, has extreme lack of control, with blood sugar that swings widely and rapidly from one extreme to the other, and so is in constant danger of insulin reaction on the one hand and acidosis on the other.

If you are a true brittle diabetic, you must follow all the rules very rigidly, checking your second urine specimen or, better, your blood four times a day so you always know exactly where your sugar level stands. You should have a reflectance meter or use the strip method (see the next chapter) so you can read your blood sugar in an instant. You may also be a candidate for an insulin pump.

Why you are unstable is a mystery in most cases, but some people are extremely sensitive to a difference of one or two units of insulin. Others, because of neuropathy, have stomachs that do not empty quickly and so glucose does not get into the bloodstream fast enough. Some have defects in their compensation mechanisms so the liver doesn't release sugar when it is needed. And perhaps there are other reasons we don't yet know about.

But, in most instances, "brittle" diabetics are not *really* brittle. They have simply never learned how to cope correctly with their condition. Perhaps their doctors have prescribed doses of insulin that are much too high. Then they eat too much to prevent reactions, thus raising their blood sugar way up, then take more insulin to bring it down, in a never-ending circle. Or perhaps they are not eating the correct diet, or have not tried taking insulin in split doses.

They may not know how to handle sick days, exercise days or days of little activity. Maybe they have been checking their urine only after fasting (in the morning before breakfast), and don't know how they are doing after a meal. If they have an excellent fasting sugar or, the opposite, a fasting sugar that is too high and then base their whole day's insulin on that, they may be taking too little or too much as a result.

Before you accept a diagnosis of "brittle," be sure you and your doctor have explored all the possibilities.

EIGHT

Testing Your Blood Sugar

ALTHOUGH there are many more enjoyable experiences in life, you must test your urine and/or blood. Testing is a diabetic's best friend because it tells you how well your body is handling the sugar it both produces internally and processes from the food you eat. It is a simple and essential procedure. You don't have to love it, but you have to do it.

All diabetics—whether their diabetes is controlled by diet alone, oral agents or insulin—must test *every day*, no matter how they feel.

Many diabetics insist they can *tell* when their sugar isn't normal. That's why they don't bother to take tests very often. If they feel "off," then they make a test. But the truth is, few people can detect sugar fluctuations unless they fall very low or rise very high. It is a rare person who will notice any true symptoms unless their blood sugar is below about 40 mgs or above 400, and some people don't notice them until their sugar goes much higher than that.

Find out for yourself. Note down your feelings, decide whether you feel normal, high or low, then test your urine and/or blood four times a day for a couple of weeks. Were you always correct? It is extremely doubtful that you were.

Why Must You Do It?

Why is testing important? Why, if you feel well, must you know your blood-sugar level? Because the effects of diabetes are cumulative, and it is well known today that consistently high or even moderately high sugar over a long period of time can help to bring about dire physical complications. It is very important that your sugar is normal most of the time because high levels of blood sugar have an eventual deleterious effect on every organ of the body.

Urine testing is an everyday affair which should be supplemented at least periodically with blood testing. The percentage of sugar spilled into your urine reflects the amount circulating in your blood a few hours ago. For a more accurate picture of what is happening internally in your bloodstream at this very moment, you need tests made on a sample of blood.

How often these are necessary must be determined by your physician and depends on your particular case. If you have diabetes that is quite stable, perhaps once every couple of months is sufficient.

If you are moderately stable, your doctor may decide you need blood tests every few weeks. And if you are a "brittle," unstable or severe diabetic, *every day or even four times a day may not be too often.* During a period of stress—illness, pregnancy, etc.—blood tests must also be made frequently, perhaps every two to four hours.

Glycosuria and Renal Thresholds

Glycosuria is sugar "spilled" into the urine, and this sugar is what is measured when you make a urine test. The nondiabetic rarely spills any sugar because his body copes with incoming sugar by secreting enough insulin to cover it. Nor is his blood sugar rarely higher than about 150 mg percent. In diabetics, however, blood sugar can rise to phenomenal heights if it is not controlled by enough insulin.

There is one hitch to urine testing, and that is your individual renal threshold. The renal threshold determines how much sugar there is in your bloodstream before it spills out into the urine. Below a certain amount (different for everyone), the blood sugar is not excreted in the urine but is passed along to other parts of the body. Normally, blood sugar must be between 150 and 180 mgs percent before you spill.

Some, usually elderly, people have high thresholds. Blood sugar may be 220 mgs or more before it passes into the urine. Therefore they will have negative urine tests even when their sugar is extremely high. Others, usually children or teenagers, have low renal thresholds and will spill even though their sugar is not elevated above normal. And a few people lack the enzyme to return the sugar to the body and so sugar is spilled continually. This is called renal diabetes.

It is important then for you to know if your renal threshold is out of the normal range. If it is, it is more difficult to use urine tests as a sign of control because a high blood-sugar level may not cause a corresponding high value in the urine. Therefore, blood tests rather than urine tests will give you much more accurate readings of your blood sugar.

For a nondiabetic, fasting blood sugar is considered to be normal at about 70 to 100 mgs percent. One hour after a meal, 100 to 140 mgs is the usual normal range, but up to 185 may still be considered acceptable. Two hours after eating, blood sugar drops to about 80 to 120 mgs (but up to 145 mgs is still normal), then continues to fall until it reaches the fasting level again.

A diabetic's blood-sugar level often goes much higher than these levels, though it is important to aim at the normal range. You must try to keep your blood-sugar level at no more than 140 mg percent fasting, and no more than 200 mg two hours after a meal. A consistent pattern of blood sugars above these levels does not bode well for your future well-being.

How Often Should Tests Be Made?

You must test your sugar level every day, whether you take medication or not. And you should keep a record of the results.

Diabetics who are controlled by diet alone and whose sugars are usually negative can probably get along well with only one urine test a day, just before going to bed. The results will tell you whether your diet requires adjustment or whether you may require medication to keep your diabetes under control.

If you take oral hypoglycemic agents, a schedule of two tests a day—before breakfast and before bed—will inform you about your control. If you are not doing well, then you must also test before lunch and dinner until you see normal results once more. You, too, must adjust your diet so that the oral agents will be sufficient to help you produce or utilize enough of your own insulin to compensate for what you eat. If you cannot do that, you may have to increase your dose or graduate to insulin injections.

If you take insulin, then tests must be made at least three times a day—before breakfast, dinner and bed. In times of stress, add a fourth test, before lunch. If this means you must test in your office or the school bathroom, you will find it easiest and less obvious to use a strip-test method (see pages 128–32). Except in rare cases, it is not usual practice to ask patients to check urine at lunchtime because of the inconvenience. Generally enough information can be gleaned from the other three daily tests to achieve good control.

Each test gives you a report on the action of your medication vs. your food consumption and exercise during the immediately preceding period of time.

No matter what kind of diabetic you are, you must make at least four tests a day if you:

Have an infection, even a cold.

Feel nauseated or weak or have diarrhea.

Lose weight.

Are very thirsty or urinate frequently.

See any unusual pattern to your test results.

Keep Records

Isolated test results won't tell you or your doctor very much, except that *at this moment* your blood sugar is high or low. But if you write down the results after each test, you will be able to detect a pattern to your blood-sugar levels and correct for any aberrations. An isolated high or low result isn't very important, but consistent highs or lows will tell you and the doctor that a change must be made. Your diet, your medication, or your activity may require adjustments, or an undiagnosed illness may need treatment.

Write your test results in a notebook, and make short notations about how you feel, whether you are ill, tired, stressed, if you have overindulged in food, underindulged in exercise, had a bad night's sleep, suffered an emotional high or low, etc.

Read over your accumulated test results once or twice a week to see if there are any recurring patterns of abnormal readings of high or low sugar levels, so you can make your own adjustments or discuss your situation with your doctor. Be sure your doctor knows which test method and method of recording you are using. The numbers or colors have different meanings depending on the test you use. In fact, it is best if you record and discuss your results in *percentages* of sugar rather than by colors or numbers, just to avoid dangerous confusion.

If You Are Sick

Make tests at least four times a day, and test for acetone if your sugar is high. Talk to your doctor at least once a day for instructions about medication based on that day's test results. See Chapter 12.

Choosing a Home Urine-Testing Method

Whatever test you and your doctor choose, you must know exactly how to use it. Wrong test results are useless, or worse, very dangerous. Ask your doctor for an explanation and also read the instructions carefully. One young patient brought me a specimen that looked too clear for urine. I said, "John, you went into the bathroom and brought me water from the sink!" He was more interested in pleasing me than controlling his diabetes. The goal of testing is not to please anyone, but to be a guide to the correct treatment to keep you in control.

There is a variety of urine-testing methods and each has its advantages and disadvantages. Some are cheaper, some are more convenient, some are contraindicated with certain other drugs. After a discussion with your doctor, you may want to try different kinds and decide which works best for you.

Unless you are instructed otherwise, always make your morning test with a *second-voided* urine specimen. This means that you urinate after arising and discard the urine, drink a glass of water, then test a second specimen passed 30 minutes later. The urine you have collected throughout the night is a mixed bag; it contains sugar that may have arrived in your bladder at any time since you went to bed. The second voiding will provide you with urine that will reflect the last few hours.

To make tests later in the day, the same rule applies. It is best to urinate about an hour before a meal, discard the urine, drink a glass of water, and test a second specimen in half an hour or an hour. This specimen won't hold the sugar that forms the first few hours after a meal and so is more likely to reflect your current blood-sugar state.

Clinitest Five-Drop: This requires a test tube and a dropper. After urinating into a cup, place 5 drops of urine in the test tube, then add 10 drops of water. Drop in a Clinitest tablet and wait 15 seconds after the bubbling stops. Now shake the tube gently. Check the color of the liquid against the color chart provided with the test kit.

Colors range from blue (negative sugar) to green to brown to orange (high sugar, 4+, or over 2%). Green indicates a trace of sugar, yellow means about 1 % or 3 +.

It is best not to trust the five-drop Clinitest method if you tend to have consistent high sugars or if the method shows your reading is very high, because when blood sugar goes higher than 2%, the increments cannot be read easily.

Color	Percent sugar	Level
Blue	0	0
Green	¼%	Trace
Cloudy green	½%	1+
Olive green	¾%	2+
Yellow to light brown	1%	3+
Orange	2%	4+
Orange to greenish brown	Over 2%	

Clinitest Two-Drop: If the five-drop method shows over 2% (4+) sugar, it is an excellent idea to follow it with the two-drop method to determine just how much higher your sugar is. Place 2 drops of urine in 10 drops of water, add a tablet, wait, then shake gently. An orange result signifies 5% sugar, or at least 5+. You may be in deep trouble if you don't cope with this kind of sugar immediately.

Color	*Percent sugar*	*Level*
Blue	0	0
Green	¼%	Trace
Cloudy green	½%	1+
Olive green	1%	2+
Yellow brown	2%	3+
Light brown	3%	4+
Orange	5%	5+

Clinitest is a simple test, though not the most convenient because it involves test tubes and tablets. But it always detects urinary sugar and its colors are easy to read—with the already-mentioned exception. If your sugar is very high, the color may "pass through" the bright orange (2% or 4+) of the five-drop test and turn brownish again. If your result is orange or brown, it is very wise to move on to the two-drop procedure.

Clinitest never gives false negative results, but it can give false positive if you take certain drugs. Among the drugs that affect Clinitest readings are NegGram (nalidixic acid) and Keflex, both commonly prescribed for urinary-tract infections. Also Probenecid for gout, large doses of vitamin C, aspirin or penicillin. You may also get false positive results if your are breast-feeding because of lactose, a form of sugar, in the urine. Switch for the duration to another test method, such as Tes-Tape or Diastix, which doesn't react to lactose.

Clinitest tablets spoil if they are exposed to moisture. Don't store them in the bathroom. Always replace the cap tightly immediately after removing a tablet. Don't put anything else in the jar or transfer the contents to another container. Don't handle the tablets. Do not expose them to excessive heat or light. Throw them out if they turn dark blue. Some tablets are foil-wrapped and will stay fresh longer.

Tes-Tape: The handiest test kit and great for travelers, this is a plastic container holding a roll of yellow paper tape. Tear off a two-inch strip of tape. Hold the tape at one end with your fingers (do not touch the other end) and dip it in your urine. Pull it out and wait exactly one minute before reading the result. Check the color against the colors on the dispenser.

If the color is unchanged (yellow), your sugar is **negative**. If the colors show $\frac{1}{2}\%$ or over, wait another minute and compare. A very dark green or blue indicates the highest sugar levels.

At high sugar levels, Tes-Tape may underread your blood sugar, jumping so quickly form $\frac{1}{2}\%$ to 2% that it may not be accurate when you reach this range. So, if you tend to spill high amounts of sugar frequently, you will be better off using the two-drop Clinitest method. This will give you a better indicator of how much you are spilling.

Caution: Do not dip into urine the part of the tape you have held in your fingers. There is enough sugar on your fingertips to cause a false positive test.

Tes-Tape is simple and uncumbersome, travels well and will never give false positive readings when you take drugs or are breast-feeding, because it only measures glucose. On the other hand, it sometimes gives false negatives with medications. Nor does it take kindly to moisture. Keep it dry or it may deteriorate. Don't handle it. It also may not be accurate if it is too old.

Color	Percent Sugar	Level
Yellow	0	0
Light green	1/10%	1+
Dark green	¼%	2+
Dark green to blue	½%	3+
Dark blue	2% or more	4+

Diastix: These plastic strips with a small blue paper square at one end are also convenient and travel well. Dip the blue square into the urine for two seconds, tap off excess. Wait 30 seconds, then check the color, which ranges from blue (negative) to brown (positive).

Diastix, like Tes-Tape, won't give false positive results though false *negatives* are possible when you take certain drugs.

Because the presence of a considerable amount of acetone in your urine can inhibit the reaction of sugar on the chemical paper square, there is a danger of underreading with Diastix. For example, you may see a 2+ color when your sugar is really 4+ if you also have acetone. Therefore, we recommend that, instead of Diastix, you use Keto-Diastix even if you are not interested in your acetone reading at this testing. See below. Besides, Keto-Diastix are longer and easier to handle.

Color	Percent sugar	Level
Blue	0	0
Light green	1/10%	Trace
Dark green	¼%	1+
Olive green	½%	2+
Light brown	1%	3+
Dark brown	2%	4+

Mega-Diastix: These are the same as Diastix but 15 times larger, so the colors are very easy to see. They are made for people who have poor vision.

Testing for Acetone

Whenever you get a high sugar reading, it is very important to test for the presence of acetones (or ketones) because, if you are producing these acids as a result of burning fat instead of carbohydrate, you *must* know it and correct it promptly. If you don't, you are setting forth on a short road to acidosis and plenty of trouble. If your urine shows acetone as well as high sugar, check with your doctor about what to do. He/she may want you to take more medication immediately or wait to see if the acetone continues to be spilled. Test for it every two to four hours until it is completely gone. See Chapter 10 for more details.

Ketostix: These are similar to Diastix. Dip the strip into the urine. Wait for 15 seconds, then compare the colors with the chart given. The acetone square will turn lavender or purple when you have acetone.

Color	Amount of Acetone
No change	None
Lavender	Small amount
Light purple	Moderate amount
Dark purple	Large amount

Acetest: Place an Acetest tablet on a clean piece of paper. Put a drop or two of urine on the tablet, using a dropper. Wait 30 seconds, then compare colors on the chart provided with each bottle of tablets. Again lavender through dark purple indicate acetone.

Keto-Diastix: These, too, are plastic strips, but longer than Diastix, which makes them easier to use. They have two squares at one end of the strip, one to indicate acetone, the other to indicate sugar. Dip the strip in the urine. Wait 15 seconds, then compare the acetone square with the chart. If you have acetone, the square will turn lavender or purple, as the chart above shows.

For the sugar reading, wait another 15 seconds (a total of 30 seconds) after dipping into the urine. The sugar-indicating square will change colors, ranging from blue to brown in the same order as Diastix.

Home Blood-Testing Methods

Blood testing gives you very specific blood-sugar readings. It tells you where you are *right now*, eliminating the time lag that is inevitable with urine testing.

Blood tests are especially helpful if you are sick, if you are a juvenile-onset diabetic who finds it hard to maintain control, or a brittle diabetic who needs constant insulin adjustment or if you are pregnant. They are also useful to people who want to check the effect of certain foods on their blood sugars. For example, if you wonder if a scoop of ice cream, or an apple, or crackers, will raise your blood sugar far out of bounds, check your sugar two hours after you have eaten them. If your blood is not abnormally elevated, you are home free (provided you have a normal renal threshold).

Because there's no immediate clinical reason to make blood tests unless you are prepared to respond to the information they give you, you must know how to adjust your medication, food and exercise accordingly. This takes study, experience and motivation, after a thorough discussion with your doctor.

Drawing a Drop of Blood

It's astonishing—or maybe it isn't—how many people are afraid to prick their fingers to get the necessary drop of blood for testing. But after you have done it a few times, you will see it isn't really traumatic. Besides, help is here for those of faint heart. In place of a lancet (which you can buy in disposable form), you may wish to use an Autolet or Penlet. These employ a spring action which releases a lancet and need only to be pressed against your fingers to prick it automatically. Most patients say this is positively painless.

Now, to get that drop of blood: Swab your finger with alcohol and let it dry. With your lancet or autolet, make a small prick and squeeze out a large drop of blood. Drop the blood onto your test strip.

You can prick any part of your fingertips but you will feel it least if you use the sides of the finger pads, because there are fewer nerve endings there. The thumb and the fourth finger are the least sensitive.

Chemstrip bG: These are chemically treated plastic strips. Draw a drop of blood and place it on a strip. Wait 60 seconds, wipe the blood off with dry cotton, wait another 60 seconds. Compare the color with the guide on the container.

If the reading is more than 240 mgs percent, wait one more minute. It may move higher.

Dextrostix: These are plastic strips similar to Diastix. Drop the blood on the strip, wait 60 seconds, then gently wash off the smear under running water or with a squeeze bottle. Pat dry with cotton or a tissue. Now compare the color with the color scale on the bottle. Colors range from cream (0 mg glucose); to moss green (25 mg); blue-green (45 mg); teal blue (90 mg); sapphire blue (130 mg); midnight blue (175 mg); purple-blue (250 mg or more). Differentiating between the shades of greens and blues can be difficult, especially in the higher ranges.

Reflectance Meters

For more accurate reading, you may want to invest in an electronic reflectance meter that will read the colors for you. The meters are not cheap, but they are tax deductible as a medical expense, and will allow you to keep close tabs on your blood sugar.

Glucoscan: A small lightweight portable machine, this gives quick accurate results. Stick your finger, place a drop of blood on the test strip, blot dry. Insert the strip into the meter, which will indicate a number. This is your blood-sugar level.

Ames Glucometer: Another lightweight and portable reflectance meter that gives excellent readings. It works in a similar way, though the strips must be washed gently before they are read by the machine. However, Glucoscan provides strips compatible with the Ames machine that require no washing.

The Test That Tells All

The urine and finger-stick blood tests we have been discussing give you important information about how good your control is today. The hemoglobin A_1c test, a blood-sugar test made in a laboratory, tells how you have been doing for the last two or three months.

Because the hemoglobin A_1c test tattles, reporting your past performance, it is especially important if you don't test often enough and tend to let your control slide. Or if you are one of those people who behave themselves for a week or so before each visit to the doctor but neglect their diabetes in between. Even though you know that consistent high sugars will cause disaster eventually, you may pay little attention until you get into trouble. This test, if it is made regularly, helps to keep you on the path to righteousness.

Hemoglobin A_1c is hemoglobin with glucose attached to it. Normally it is only a tiny part of your total hemoglobin supply. But when you have elevated blood sugar, the glucose tends to stick to the hemoglobin A that makes up 97.5 percent of your red blood cells. The more sugar in your blood, the more saturated the hemoglobin A becomes. Once the cells have glucose attached to them, the sugar remains there throughout their lifespan—about 120 days.

By measuring the A_1c, your doctor will know your overall blood-sugar level during the last couple of months. A normal level ranges between 4 to 7 percent (depending on the methods used by the laboratory). A level higher than that indicates the need for prompt reform.

This test does not require fasting or repeated sampling, nor need it be done at any special time of day. It would be wise to have it made about every six months. Meantime, don't forget your daily home tests.

Note: Occasionally, the hemoglobin A_1c test fails to give accurate or useful results. The reason could be that it hasn't been made within the correct time limits or at a reliable laboratory; or the results could be skewed by wide swings in your blood-sugar levels just before undergoing the test. However, in almost all cases it is an excellent indication of your control for the last couple of months.

NINE

Insulin Reactions

Wʜᴇɴ you are an insulin-taking diabetic, you quickly learn that you have a major concern which hardly anybody else ever worries about or knows exists. That's insulin reaction, very low blood sugar (hypoglycemia) caused by the presence of too much insulin in your bloodstream. Unless you are always spilling sugar (a bad idea), it is inevitable that you will have an occasional reaction, usually minor and easily handled. While reactions can hardly be described as delightful experiences, they are far healthier than having consistently high blood sugar, which in time can do inexorable damage to your body.

Besides, reactions can usually be avoided, and certainly minimized, by using your comon sense.

In the nondiabetic, insulin is produced by the islet cells of the pancreas in response to the level of sugar in the bloodstream. The amount is always just enough to cover the sugar, and there is never too much. If the blood-glucose level falls too low, the liver releases more sugar from its standby stores, again just the right amount to do the job.

But diabetics who require exogenous insulin do not run on "automatic." They must try to match the amount of insulin they take with the blood sugar they *expect* to have. Sometimes, for various reasons, they have too much insulin in their bloodstream, and the blood-sugar level falls too low. When this happens, the brain and the central nervous system do not have the glucose they need for fuel and start to function less efficiently. The result is an insulin reaction.

Diet Therapy or Oral Agents

If you are a diabetic who is treated with diet alone, you will *never* have insulin reactions. If you take oral agents, there is a remote possibility of reactions under certain rare circumstances, but so remote that I have seen only a few in twenty-five years of practice. As we have discussed, they occur in most cases only when there is a change in liver or kidney function, or when the diabetic is elderly and frail, or is seriously ill and eats so poorly that he does not have an adequate store of glycogen ready to be released from the liver in emergencies.

Warnings and Symptoms

For an insulin-dependent diabetic, the possibility of a reaction begins when blood sugar falls below 40 or 50 mgs percent. Or when sugar makes a sudden nose dive, even if it goes from 400 to 200 mgs percent. The exact level as well as the symptoms vary for everyone.

Early warnings that a reaction is happening may include one or more of these feelings: weakness, sweating, head-

ache, nausea, sudden hunger, anxiety, confusion, clumsi-
ness, shakiness, pallor, palpitations, tingling of the lips,
dizziness, a change in attitude, such as inappropriate laugh-
ing or crying. Most of these sensations result from the
adrenaline (epinephrine) hormones your body pours into
the bloodstream in an effort to raise your blood sugar.

Sometimes a headache is the only sign. Sometimes the
feeling of being very tired for no particular reason is the
sole warning signal. When this happens, don't go to sleep
without checking to see if your urine is negative. If it is,
you are probably starting to have a reaction.

Some people become very irritable, even hostile and ag-
gressive, when their sugar is very low. Others find their vision becomes blurred.

If the reaction is allowed to continue, the symptoms may
progress to slurred speech, mental confusion, dilated pu-
pils, instability and eventually to convulsions and loss of
consciousness. A good rule for all insulin-taking diabetics:
Before driving, count backward from 100 by sevens. It you
can't do it, take sugar immediately.

What Causes Reactions?

The low blood sugar that leads to a reaction is caused by
just three things:

Taking too much insulin (sometimes by mistake).

Not eating when and what you should.

Exercising more than usual without compensating with
extra calories or less insulin.

Reactions usually happen just before a meal, or when
your insulin has its peak effect. See Chapter 7.

Are Reactions Harmful?

Most experts agree that mild reactions don't hurt you. And
that, unless a reaction is very severe and prolonged, with

an extended state of unconsciousness and perhaps amnesia, they won't do any permanent damage.

Prevention is Common Sense

If you know what triggers reactions, then you can almost always avoid them or head them off quickly.

• Always eat *on time* and eat *enough*. Never skip a meal unless you take less insulin. Don't forget your scheduled snacks.

• Be extremely careful when you measure out your insulin. Don't switch strengths (only one strength—U-100—will soon be available in the U.S., but other strengths are sold in other countries), and always use the syringe that matches your strength.

• If you are going to do more exercise than usual, eat more slow-acting carbohydrate (starch) in preparation for it, or take less insulin, or both. See Chapter 5. Consult with your doctor to determine amounts. Before you set out to exercise, always test your urine—or, better yet, your blood—for sugar. If it is negative before you even begin, then you surely need to make adjustments.

Watch for reactions the day *after* heavy exercise, when your liver may still be depleted of its supply of extra glycogen. Your food, which normally would go into blood sugar, is now funneled into your liver to be stored, so you may need more food (or less insulin) in order to prevent hypoglycemia. Besides, you have increased your number of insulin receptor sites by exercising.

During your exercise, especially if it is strenuous and prolonged, it is quite possible you need some additional sugar. (Most people don't think of sex as exercise, but it is. Eat a snack before jumping into bed.)

• Sometimes, perhaps on a Saturday or Sunday, you may

sleep late, skip breakfast. Since you are only going to eat two meals that day, be sure to take less insulin.

• An occasional reaction is nothing to be concerned about but if yours happen frequently, then you are doing something wrong. Usually the answer is that your insulin dosage is too high, or you are not eating enough at the right times. Review your diet and make sure you are eating a consistent number of calories that include the correct amount of carbohydrates. Check out your snacks. Are you getting enough carbohydrate and protein? There is *always* a reason for frequent reactions and you must find it.

Sometimes reactions tend to occur at the same time of day or night. Then you will know, *if you are eating correctly,* that your dose should be reevaluated and adjusted. Too much Regular insulin taken in the morning often causes reactions before lunch. Too much NPH or Lente may precipitate afternoon reactions when their action peaks. Your dose may be too high. Or you may do better with split amounts, giving you smaller but more frequent doses. Let your doctor know about your reactions and request that you review your dose, your diet and your exercise together. If you continue to have problems, perhaps you should go to another doctor, one whose specialty is diabetes.

Other Possibilities

• The rate of absorption of the insulin you inject is affected by *where* you inject it. We know that the abdomen and arms usually have higher and faster absorption rates than the legs. If your reactions tend to occur after you have used these sites, maybe this is the reason. You can use this information to your advantage, not only to explain and prevent reactions, but to help you overcome high sugars more rapidly. When your sugar is 3 or 4 +, injecting in your abdomen or arm can bring it down more rapidly.

• Pregnancy has a tremendous effect on your insulin needs (see Chapter 14), and you will probably require much less insulin in the first trimester (first 13 weeks) when the fetus and the placenta consume a lot of your circulating sugar and when you may not be eating as much as you usually do. This is a time when reactions are very common and can be severe. During the rest of your pregnancy, you will undoubtedly require much *more* insulin than usual. But after the baby is born, your insulin needs will drop again—another time when you must be especially alert to the possibility of insulin reactions.

• The insulin requirements of menstruating women can be variable, too. Certain women need more or less insulin at some point during their cycle, usually the week *before* the period.

• Your emotional state can affect your need for more or less insulin. Though chronic stress seems to raise blood sugar, acute stress can lower it in a hurry, causing a reaction.

• Vomiting or diarrhea may deplete your body of the sugar it needs to function. You must get sugar somehow to avoid a reaction, so if you can't eat, drink regular (not diet) ginger ale for nourishment, take an antiemetic in suppository form or by injection. And *immediately* call your doctor. You may need intravenous glucose if nothing else does the job. See Chapter 12.

• Too much alcohol consumption, too, can be the reason for insulin reactions, because it inhibits the release of glucose from the liver when you need it. Not only that, it may make you forget to eat on time.

• Certain drugs can have an effect on your insulin requirements. For example, Inderal, prescribed for hypertension, reduces the liver's ability to make new glucose when you need it and the result may be severe and prolonged reactions. Besides, it can mask the reactions so you won't be aware you're about to have one. Diabetics with high blood pressure seem to do better with other beta blockers, such as Lopressor or Tenormin.

• A caution for sauna devotees: A study has found that a sauna following your insulin injection can increase the absorption rate by 110 percent. So, have your sauna *after* a meal or snack, take along some carbohydrate, and since you won't be wearing your pants or carrying your wallet card, be sure to wear your ID bracelet or necklace.

• Reactions can cause blurred vision and dizziness, so take special care when you're driving or operating machinery. Be sure your blood sugar isn't too low before you start, and have a snack every half hour or so if you stay at it for a long time. Remember the suggestion of counting backward from 100 by sevens.

• Hot or very cold weather also seem to affect some people's sugar metabolism because more energy is expended, especially when the extreme temperatures are combined with exercise. Be on the alert for reactions.

Nighttime Reactions

Many people, especially before their insulin dosage is adjusted properly, have reactions during the night or in the early morning. If this is the case with you, you should always, without fail, remember to eat a snack before bedtime. If there is no reason to suspect the hypoglycemia is caused by more exercise than usual that day or less food than you normally consume, *then your answer lies in your insulin dose.* You are taking too much Intermediate- or long-acting insulin in the morning. Decrease it by about 4 units and see if the nighttime reactions stop. If your daytime sugars go higher as a result, then a small amount of

Regular insulin can be added to the syringe in the morning. Make changes in your dose only after consulting your doctor.

Know Your Blood Sugar

Diabetics who take insulin must test their urine or blood a few times a day. If you keep a record of your sugars, you will be able to tell if there is a pattern to your episodes of hypoglycemia. You'll know if they seem to be caused by specific happenings in your life. You will also know when you must eat more or take less insulin so you won't have reactions.

Blood sugars, because they tell you what is happening in your bloodstream *now* rather than reflecting your condition a few hours ago are more helpful than urine tests in making an assessment of your current situation. If you tend to have many reactions, it would be a wise investment to buy a reflectance meter (see Chapter 8) to help you interpret quickly and correctly the results of finger-stick blood tests. A cheaper method, almost as good, is the Chemstrip bG test.

When you know exactly where your blood sugar stands at any given moment, you can start to plan small adjustments in your eating or insulin schedules as needed.

React to a Reaction Fast

If you suspect you are beginning to have a reaction, don't wait around to see what's going to happen. Don't fight it. Do something right *now*. You may not have much time before you are in real trouble. Even if you are not sure that what you feel is a reaction, even if you think perhaps these symptoms may be caused by high sugar rather than low and you don't have the time or the facilities to test your blood sugar immediately, take preventive measures. In this case, better safe than sorry really applies.

Treatment at this stage is easy. Eat something. If the reaction is mild, some carbohydrate and protein (perhaps a glass of milk and some crackers) is sufficient. If it seems more pronounced or you tend to have reactions that come upon you quickly, take rapidly absorbed sugar: 2 teaspoons of granulated sugar—plain or dissolved in a little water; 6 or 7 Lifesavers or hard candies; 4 ounces of orange juice or regular (not diet) soft drink; 2 teaspoons of honey or corn syrup; a handful of raisins; whatever is handy and appeals to you most.

Some diabetics carry little tubes of "Instant Glucose" with them. This is 25 grams of concentrated sugar that can be squeezed right into your mouth and absorbs very quickly (order it from the Diabetes Association of Cleveland, 2022 Lee Road, Cleveland, Ohio 44118). A similar product is Reactose or Glutose, available in pharmacies or through your ADA affiliate.

Don't overshoot the mark and take so much sugar that you will pay for it later in high blood sugar. You need 10 or 15 or, at most, 20 grams of sugar. After you have taken the sugar, *wait.* It takes 10 or 15 minutes for it to be absorbed into the bloodstream and reach your brain. If you don't start to feel better after 15 minutes, eat more.

Some people are so frightened of reactions that they start eating and keep on eating until the feelings have passed. By then they have so overdosed that it takes them days to get their blood sugar down to normal again. It is like killing a fly with a .22 rifle. Most effective in preventing rebound high sugars is a glass of milk with two crackers. Wait 15 minutes and repeat if necessary.

Obviously, the fuel you may need in a hurry must always be readily available to you. Carry some supplies in your pocket or handbag at all times, in the car's glove compartment, your suitcase, the desk drawer. One man keeps his in the top of his sock when he runs; another ties a little bag of sugar packets to his belt. No matter where you stash it, your emergency supplies must literally be at hand.

Important: Make a frequent check on your cache of sweets. Somebody else may have eaten them! Or perhaps you used them and forgot to stock up again.

Back to Your Normal Schedule

After you have taken extra food in response to a reaction, do not cut back on your regular eating plan. Forget you had it and eat as usual. That sugar is not to be calculated as part of your daily diet.

Your blood sugar will "rebound" within about an hour after treating a reaction with sugar, sometimes going as high as 200 or 300 mgs. Don't take extra insulin to counteract it, but test your urine again before your next meal.

Reactions Without Warning

You may be one of those diabetics who, after having had the disease for many years, tend to get reactions without any warning at all. If so, you must try even harder to avoid them. Test your urine or blood four times a day. Be sure to have snacks at 10:30 AM., 3:30 P.M., and before you go to bed, whether or not you think you need them. Include in your bedtime snack some protein (i.e., cheese or milk) as well as carbohydrate. During the night, your body will slowly convert that protein to usable carbohydrate.

What Other People Should Know

Just in case you ever have a severe reaction and can't respond to it yourself, train your family, responsible friends and colleagues to know what to do. If you are in school, your teachers should know. Tell them that if you are conscious, they should give you the quickly absorbed sweets described above, even if you object. Your low sugar when you have a reaction may make you stubborn!

If you are unconscious, that is another story. Nothing should be forced into your mouth because you may aspirate it. Now you will require an injection of glucagon and you will be wise to keep this handy, too, especially if you are prone to sudden and severe reactions. It requires a prescription and is available at drugstores.

The glucagon comes, with instructions, in a kit containing two ampules, one holding a powder, the other a liquid. Using your insulin syringe, your helper should inject the liquid into the powdered glucagon, pull out the needle and shake the ampule to dissolve the powder. Then withdraw the solution with the syringe and inject it anywhere under the skin. It is extremely rare that one injection does not solve the problem of extreme hypoglycemia. It will probably bring you around in about 10 minutes and now you can take sugar by mouth. But if you don't respond, a second shot will not be effective. You must be seen by a doctor immediately or taken to a hospital emergency room for intravenous glucose infusion or other treatment.

Be sure someone in your family, at school or work, knows how to give glucagon injections. It is very simple and requires no medical knowledge or expertise.

The Difference Between Insulin Reaction and Acidosis

Because acidosis, which we will discuss in the next chapter, can also lead to coma, it is sometimes difficult for you or another layperson to know the difference when you begin to feel peculiar or actually pass out. When in doubt, however, treat yourself for a reaction if you haven't the time to take a test, because insulin shock can lay you out very quickly. Diabetic coma happens gradually.

The best indication of an insulin reaction is profuse sweating, as opposed to acidosis when you hardly sweat at all. In acidosis, even your tongue and your armpits, a heavy source of sweat glands, will be dry because you have lost so much water in excessive urination.

Of course, the best way to know whether your sugar is low or high is to make a quick blood test, if you have time. A Dextrostix, Chemstrip or Glucoscan strip and a drop of blood from your finger (see Chapter 8) will tell you immediately what your status is.

Label Yourself

Not only should you let everyone with whom you associate know you are a diabetic who may have reactions, but it is most important to wear or carry something that identifies you as a diabetic—a bracelet, a necklace, and/or a wallet card that explains who you are and what to do. It will let people know how to act in an emergency, and will help keep you out of the local jail where many diabetics land when their behavior or lack of consciousness is misinterpreted as overindulgence in alcoholic spirits.

TEN

Coping with Acidosis

Though the exclusive rights to insulin reactions belong almost entirely to diabetics who take insulin, this is not the case with acidosis, at the other end of the blood-sugar spectrum. No matter what kind of diabetic you are and whether or not you take insulin, you are not immune to this complication, which is caused by too little insulin and too much sugar in your bloodstream.

Any diabetic can go into acidosis with continued poor control or a sudden stress such as an illness or injury. Not only that, but acidosis is not a benign complication. If it is allowed to progress into diabetic coma, it can endanger your health and even your life if it is untreated.

But acidosis has one virtue; it doesn't happen suddenly. It develops gradually, usually over a few days. Even in the case of some juvenile or brittle diabetics, it takes about 12 to 24 hours. High sugar and acetone will show up in your urine tests. This gives you time, if you are paying attention, to prevent serious consequences. If you take urine or blood tests every day and have learned to recognize the symptoms, you will always know when you are in danger of acidosis and so you can take appropriate measures.

If you have a high renal threshold (see Chapter 8), which means sugar does not spill into the urine as it normally does when the blood sugar reaches about 160 mgs percent, you will need to test your *blood* rather than your urine at frequent intervals to be sure you do not have the high sugar levels that will lead to acidosis.

What Is It?

Acidosis is a condition that results from hyperglycemia, too *much* sugar in the blood. In most cases, when the body lacks sufficient insulin to metabolize sugar, it starts burning its own fat and protein tissue for fuel. This emergency fuel produces acetone and other ketones, fatty acids that are released into the bloodstream, changing its chemistry to an acid state.

If acidosis isn't checked, coma and eventually death are the end results. Acidosis is *serious*. Happily, the current emphasis on good control and frequent tests have made it a much less common event than it used to be.

The Warning Signs

You must act quickly as soon as you notice any signs of acidosis. What are the signs? The first is high blood sugar, the reason you must test your urine and/or blood *every day*.

When your blood sugar increases without enough insulin to handle it, you will have the same symptoms that may have led you to go to the doctor when your diabetes was diagnosed. You will start spilling sugar into your urine. You will have to urinate frequently as the body tries to rid itself of the sugar, and will soon become dehydrated and extremely thirsty. Your skin will be dry. Your tongue will be dry. You may start to lose weight, your vision may be dim or blurred. Your breath, because you are burning fat instead of carbohydrate, may smell fruity or sweet like peaches or violets or freshly mowed hay.

Now, if you still don't acknowledge what's going on and deal with it, you will start to feel nauseated and perhaps develop abdominal pains. These symptoms will progress to a flushed face, labored breathing, drowsiness, disorientation and eventually loss of consciousness.

What Causes Acidosis?

The most common causes of acidosis are omitting your insulin or having an infection. It can also be precipitated by poor control (whether or not you take insulin), incorrect diet, failing to watch your blood-sugar levels with the proper vigilance and then not responding to high sugars immediately. Preventing and dealing with abnormal sugar is a diabetic's Number One job.

Sometimes you may not realize you are raising your blood sugar by eating too much of certain foods. In the summertime, for example, every doctor sees diabetics who have gone off the deep end with excessive amounts of fruit juices or raw fruits that are on their diet plan but not in the quantity in which they are consumed.

Illness, especially infection, dramatically increases your need for insulin, and is frequently the reason for an episode of high sugar and acidosis. *Be sure to take your insulin or pills when you are sick,* even though you are eating less or not at all. The fact is, you probably will need even *more* insulin, a situation you can judge only by making tests at regular close intervals. See Chapter 12 on coping with sick days.

Certain medications, such as Prednisone and Dilantin, can aggravate your diabetes, raise your blood sugar and cause you to require more insulin. These drugs can cause a condition usually seen only in elderly diabetics. It is called hyperosmolar neoketotic coma, with extremely high blood sugar but no acetone to tip you off in advance. So be sure your doctor takes your diabetes into account when prescribing any additional drugs. This advice applies to all diabetics, whether or not you take insulin.

Sometimes you may not be taking the right amount of insulin or oral agent; you can tell this from your test results and should report to your doctor. You may forget to take your medication, fail to get your proportions correct if you take split doses, use insulin whose potency has been affected by freezing or excessive heat.

But, no matter the reason for your high sugar and even if acidosis has already begun, you still have time to turn the tide.

By the way, don't take your pills with juice—it raises your blood sugar. Use water instead.

What You Should Do Now

• Call your doctor the minute your tests show high sugar and acetone, or high sugar and the symptoms of thirst and urination.

• Check your urine and/or blood *every two hours* when you see acetone.

• Take additional Regular insulin every two hours, or as instructed by your doctor, if your tests are highly positive. If you cannot reach your doctor immediately, a safe dose of Regular insulin is 20 percent (one fifth) of your usual morning dose of Intermediate-acting insulin. For example, if you normally take 40 units of NPH or Lente in the morning, add 1/5 of 40 units—or 8 units—of *Regular* insulin. If you don't normally take insulin, start taking 5 to 10 units of Regular every two hours until your blood sugar level is improved.

• Continue to take tests every two hours, and take additional Regular insulin if your tests show high sugar and acetone.

• Do *not* take extra insulin but just your usual dose if your sugar is *negative* even though acetone is present. This means the acetone has not been entirely washed out of the body (it may remain about 24 hours after the sugar has been regulated), or that you have not eaten at least 50 to 100 grams of carbohydrate in your daily diet. Now is the time to eat or drink carbohydrate to provide glucose for fuel instead of fat.

• Rest, do not exercise.

• Drink as much fluid as you can to replace what you have lost, but don't drink excessive amounts of juices or soft drinks with a high sugar content.

• Keep in close touch with your doctor. Don't be afraid to bother him/her because if you let yourself go into coma, you will be much more bother than you are now. Extreme acidosis requires that you go to the hospital for treatment. If your doctor recommends hospitalization, don't resist. Your sugar and acetone levels must be brought down to safety—fast.

Remember the Three "T's"

If you keep on top of your diabetes, you will never reach a state of serious acidosis or coma. In my twenty-five-year practice, with patients of all ages and all degrees of intelligence, I have rarely had to admit patients into the hospital for diabetic coma. That's because of the stress on tight control and three rigid rules:

1. Test your urine every day; every two hours if you have high sugar and acetone. If sugar remains persistently high, add finger-stick blood tests.
2. Telephone your doctor.
3. Take extra insulin if you need it.

ELEVEN

Worries, Worries, Worries: The Chances of Diabetic Complications

I F you live a good long life (and there's little reason to-day to expect you won't), you may eventually meet up with what is known as "diabetic complications." Diabetes is a metabolic condition with cumulative effects on the various systems of the body, so the longer you have it the more likely it is that these effects will show up.

While that is true, there is strong evidence today that the incidence and severity of the complications are closely correlated with diabetic control. That's why you should know about these possible long-term effects right from the start, long before there is the slightest sign of them. It is vi-tally important, even crucial, to your future well-being to maintain your blood sugar at a near-normal level as much of the time as you possibly can.

The "Ostrich Syndrome"

Unfortunately, many diabetic newcomers refuse to think about their unwelcome ailment, won't accept it, succumb to the "ostrich syndrome." As long as they don't have insulin reactions too often or lapse into comas and land in the hospital with regularity, they think they are doing just fine. Meantime, they don't monitor their carbohydrate intake or check their urines, and the constant high level of sugar circulating throughout the tissues of their bodies is having its inexorable effect. This happens often with "mild" diabetics who, because they take little or no medication, think they needn't be concerned and test their urines very seldom.

While many diabetic complications can be adequately treated medically, it is obviously much better to avoid them in the first place if you can. The best way to do that is to remain as close as you can to ideal control, starting *early* in your life as a diabetic.

And, if you do begin to develop any of the typical complications, to get on their case promptly. Picking them up early means avoiding many of the possible problems. If you wait until they have had a good start, reversing them may be difficult. Be sure your doctor watches for them, tests for them regularly. Don't be afraid to ask about them or to insist on the proper checkups. Report any signs or symptoms the minute you notice them.

To some degree, diabetes eventually affects all the organs and systems of the body. Many of the medical problems of diabetics are no different from those other people have, but occur more often and earlier. Some simply accelerate the natural normal aging process, especially in the large blood vessels and the connective tissue. But others are quite special to diabetes, and occur because of specific changes in the smaller blood vessels and nervous system.

Much depends on the length of time you have had diabetes, the age you were when diagnosed, your race and your gender and whether or not you are insulin-dependent. Obviously, if you live long enough—diabetics tend to live to a ripe old age today—you are susceptible to more chronic problems, especially when you have a systemic condition. Besides, the longer you have diabetes, the more chance you have of acquiring any of the complications associated with it.

The more you know about diabetes, the fewer problems you will have, because you will understand the importance of good control. Here are the pertinent facts about this collection of possible long-term diabetic complications.

Heart Attacks, Strokes and Arteriosclerosis

Arteriosclerosis, narrowing of the large blood vessels, is to be expected by all of us as we grow older. Coronary heart disease is the single largest cause of death in the United States today. Diabetics certainly don't own exclusive rights to it, but they do comprise a disproportionate percentage of the population to have it. As a group, diabetics develop arteriosclerosis, especially in the heart, head and legs, much more often and earlier—perhaps a decade or so— than nondiabetics. It's been estimated by the United States Public Health Service that, while cardiovascular disease accounts for death among 50 percent of the general population, it is the cause of death for 75 percent of diabetics, who are twice as likely to have coronary heart disease, twice as likely to have strokes, and five times as likely to have arterial disease of the extremities.

One of the reasons for this situation is that diabetics have a predisposition towards hyperlipidemia, an abnormally high amount of fats circulating in the bloodstream rather than being stored. This leads to the accumulation of deposits of fatty substances on the inner walls of the major blood vessels. The thought today is that your genetic makeup, what you eat, and how efficient your insulin supply is, are all important factors.

People with diabetes tend to be overweight and to have high blood pressure, two conditions that can aggravate cardiovascular problems. Obesity requires extra blood supply to nourish the extra body tissue, and puts it own strain on the heart as well. High blood pressure means an obvious stress on all the blood vessels, including the heart.

So What Can I Do?

Since you know you have a tendency to develop cardiovascular complications earlier and more rapidly than other people, your job is to try to head them off. First, of course, as always, you must maintain good diabetic control, not just today and for a few days next month, but constantly. The less sugar circulating throughout your body the better.

If you are overweight, it is essential to lose weight. As you lose, you will see dramatic improvements in your blood triglyceride levels and—a most important feature—a drop in your blood pressure if it is high. Because high blood pressure always multiplies the risk of heart attack and stroke, you must bring it down with diet or, if necessary, medication.

Be sure your doctor is aware that you are diabetic. This may sound ridiculous—of course, your doctor knows—but if you use different doctors for different ailments, that may not be the case. Or he/she may forget for the moment. Some medications such as Inderal, designed to reduce blood pressure, can be dangerous for diabetics and this should be noted.

A Bad Match: Diabetes and Smoking

Smoking causes arterial spasms and is definitely a habit that must go. Diabetes and smoking combine to increase the chances of heart disease many times. A diabetic, who already has a tendency toward coronary disease, needs to have everything going for him. Arterial spasms constrict the blood vessels, decreasing blood supply to the extremities—not a good idea, especially in your case. Besides, smoking may increase your chances of developing retinopathy and vision problems.

Because there is little controversy today over whether low cholesterol diets have an effect on your arteries, it is an excellent idea to limit the amount of saturated fats you eat and to increase the proportion of polyunsaturated varieties. If your cholesterol level is elevated, there are medications that your doctor may prescribe to help bring the lipid levels down to normal. Be aware that these drugs may increase your chances of gallstones and, in some people, retinal hemorrhage, and they also may affect the action of oral antidiabetic agents (see page 92).

Your cholesterol level can be evaluated by the amount of high-density lipoproteins (HDL) it contains vs. the amount of very low-density lipoproteins (VLDL). The more high-density you have, the less chance there is that you will develop hardening of the arteries after age fifty. Exercise has been found to increase HDL, and so has an alcoholic drink or two before dinner. If your cholesterol value is below 150, it is not important to know what your HDL level is. It won't be high enough to matter. And when your cholesterol exceeds 350, it's too high to bother separating out. At this point, your HDL level is rarely sufficient to protect you from arteriosclerosis. Between those two extremes, however, knowing your blood's HDL content can be useful.

As Always, Stay in Control

If you already have arteriosclerosis, you should do your best to avoid insulin reactions. That's because severe reactions are thought to put additional stress on the already narrowed blood vessels supplying the heart or the brain. However, this isn't as important as doctors have thought in the past. In fear of shocks, they have often allowed their patients to consistently spill too much sugar. Today the thinking is that reactions do not pose a great danger and that it is much more important to control blood sugar closely, even with the risk of a few reactions. In the long run, good control is best.

Next, exercise. Everyone's cardiovascular system benefits from regular exercise, especially exercise that gets the heart pumping and the lungs expanding. If you get enough (always under the supervision of your doctor), you can significantly lower your risk of heart attack. Exercise can slow your heart rate, lower your blood pressure, help burn up calories, cut down low-density lipid levels, and as an added bonus, help keep your diabetes under control by allowing you to handle carbohydrates more efficiently.

The Aspirin Treatment

Studies are currently evaluating the use of aspirin for vascular disease because of its anti-clotting effect. In addition, research has shown that it sometimes lowers blood sugar and may help prevent eye changes.

The answers are not yet in. In the meantime, it won't hurt to take a tablet (5 grains) of aspirin a day. Check with your physician—if you have retinopathy associated with hemorrhaging, or a tendency toward bleeding ulcers, it is *not* a good idea to take aspirin regularly.

The Chances of Eye Problems

This is a subject you probably would rather not discuss, but surely, as with every other diabetic ever diagnosed, it creeps into your thoughts now and then, especially in the small hours of the morning when worries are worst. There was a time, not long ago, when all diabetics had a good chance of developing vision problems, but that has drastically changed in recent years. Though it is true that diabetes is still a leading cause of blindness, there is a 90-per-cent-or-better chance it's not going to happen to you. And the odds are improving every day because of intensive research now underway.

Today we have excellent methods of coping with the typical diabetic eye changes. And we know that, with good diabetic control, especially in the first five years, you are much less likely to develop eventual difficulties. There are exceptions to every rule, of course, but, in general, people whose blood sugars are kept consistently below a certain level tend to show many fewer complications of all kinds.

Maturity-onset (NIDDM) diabetics are not as likely to develop serious eye changes as those who have the juvenile variety (IDDM); black women are in a higher risk category; and people treated by diet alone or oral agents have less chance of eye complications than those who are dependent on insulin.

Nine out of 10 diabetics, within 20 years, show some vascular changes in their retinas, the linings of the backs of the eyes where light is received and then sent to the brain for interpretation. Called background retinopathy, these early changes usually appear and then stay pretty much as they are, or sometimes clear up spontaneously and cause no problems with vision. Of the 90 percent whose eyes show these signs after 20 years, only about one in five will progress to the next set of complications called proliferative retinopathy or retinitis proliferans. This is a more precarious situation, but even among people in this group, blindness can, in most cases, be prevented.

So, while this is definitely a concern, it is far from inevitable and it gives you excellent reason to keep your blood-sugar levels within acceptable boundaries. Temporary lapses into high levels, which happen to everyone, aren't what we are talking about. It is the consistent lack of good control that is much more likely to cause trouble later in your life.

What is Background Retinopathy?

The retina is furnished with a network of tiny capillaries. After a number of years of diabetes, the walls (the basement membranes) of these blood vessels are affected, cutting down the oxygen supply to the eyes. They may then become weakened and form little bulges called microaneurysms. These, like any balloons, tend to have fragile walls and may leak serum inside the retina. Sometimes, too, they rupture and little hemorrhages occur in the backs of the eyes.

The doctor who examines your eyes looks for these microaneurysms, which show up as red dots, as well as small collections of soft, cottony or yellowish fatty material which are actually cholesterol deposits and are called exudates. If you have them, you have background retinopathy, which does not mean things will get worse. This will probably become merely a chronic condition which your diabetologist and ophthalmologist must check periodically. You probably will not even be aware of it and it will not affect your vision unless it occurs around the macula, a very small area responsible for your central vision.

What's To Be Done About It?

The very first thing you can do about retinopathy and your diabetes is to stop kidding yourself. If you don't maintain very good control over your blood-sugar levels, you are opening yourself up for a great many problems. Numerous studies have shown that sugar levels are closely linked with eye changes, all of them pointing to the importance of keeping the sugar within the normal range (below 140 mgs fasting and below 200 mgs two hours after eating).

This is not to say that maintaining perfect control (which is impossible anyway) over many years will absolutely ward off eye complications. Some people take excellent care of themselves and keep their blood sugars very close to normal, yet still develop retinopathy, while others who are wildly out of control never have it. But, as a rule, the majority of diabetics who maintain good control will not have retinopathy, while the majority of those do who not monitor their sugar levels carefully will develop eye complications. This includes all diabetics on insulin, oral agents or even diet alone.

The second thing you can do if you have background retinopathy is to be sure your blood pressure is within the normal range. Hypertension, even without diabetes, can cause retinopathy because the little blood vessels in the eyes are under stress. The combination of the two ailments obviously is undesirable. And, since smokers have a higher incidence of retinopathy, smoking, for this among many other reasons, is not acceptable for you as a diabetic.

An Eye Checkup Every Three Months

Be certain your doctor examines your eyes at *every* visit (you should see your doctor at least every three months), and *remind* him/her, if necessary, to do so. If this chore doesn't seem very important to the person you have chosen as your physician, it might be a good idea to find another. The minute the doctor sees signs of retinopathy, you should promptly see an ophthalmologist (an M.D. with a specialty in opthalmology—not an optician or an optometrist) and then return for checkups *at least* every six months.

In fact, you should see this specialist initially just after your diagnosis as a diabetic, especially if you have the maturity-onset variety of diabetes. You may have had asymptomatic diabetes for years before the diagnosis and it is an excellent idea to check your eyes out now.

Even without any eye changes, it's most important to see the ophthalmologist at least once a year. Do not wait for any sudden decreased vision or strange symptoms to make your first appointment, or even for your doctor to see evidence of microaneurysms. With the use of a special fluorescent dye, diabetic eye changes can be discovered by a specialist even earlier.

And Proliferative Retinopathy?

Retinitis proliferans is more serious than background retinopathy. It's important to know that, if treatment is going to be useful, you must start *early*. That means *right now*, just as soon as it is diagnosed. A study of 847 cases of retinitis proliferans at the Joslin Clinic, in which I participated, showed that it takes 17.4 years, on average, for a juvenile diabetic who is going to have this condition to develop it; and 4.3 years, on the average, for a person over sixty. Your doctor should be aware of the natural history of this complication.

Only about 40 percent of people who already have retinitis proliferans report to their physicians that they have noticed changes in vision or are experiencing symptoms like streaks or flashes. This means the other 60 percent with serious eye changes do not have the signals or are not acknowledging them. That is why it is vital for your doctor always to check the backs of your eyes.

Retinitis proliferans works like this: the capillaries along the inner surfaces of the retina start multiplying or proliferating, probably as a response to decreased oxygen supply to the eye. These new blood vessels try to bring more oxygen into the area, just as fire hoses bring water to a fire, but they are very fragile. They break easily and then may bleed into the retina and the vitreous, the gel-like substance that fills the eyeball. This makes the vitreous murky, preventing the passage of light from the lens to the retina. Fortunately, the blood is often reabsorbed spontaneously and the vitreous clears again.

In some cases of retinitis proliferans, the rapid growth of new and delicate blood vessels and the resulting bleeding stimulates the formation of fibrous scar tissue that can lead to a detached retina. Retinitis proliferans can also lead to a form of glaucoma which can be difficult to treat. All of this usually comes about quite slowly. If the proliferation happens only on the periphery of the retina and the vitreous isn't clouded, vision won't be seriously affected. But if it covers the central portion of the retina, if the retina starts to detach or if the vitreous becomes opaque, then we have problems. But even then, we have some solutions.

What Is the Treatment?

Several exciting new treatments have been developed and perfected in the last few years, with others on the way. One of these is photocoagulation, which involves the use of a concentrated light beam—a laser—aimed at the leaking blood vessels. The beam, which is usually painless, destroys the unwanted fragile capillaries and seals them off, resulting in harmless scar tissue. The laser is also used to shoot pinpoint blasts around the periphery of leaky eye tissue, closing off these outer capillaries to decrease the eye's oxygen requirements. Now the available blood will go to the central and most important area of the retina. Sometimes, the laser beam is used to glue the retina back in place. Photocoagulation has, in only a few years, become a major tool of the ophthalmologist and often manages to stop retinal damage right in its tracks. Lasers can also treat diabetic glaucoma, and New York opthalmologist Dr. Frances L'Esperance has developed a revolutionary method using a carbon dioxide laser.

A procedure called *vitrectomy* is another important new treatment for eyes seriously affected by retinitis proliferans. If the vitreous inside the eyeball has become clouded with little bits of leaking blood, or if it has started to contract because of the bleeding and to pull on the retina threatening to detach it, this technique may be employed to improve the situation. A special precision instrument bores a tiny hole into the eye and suctions out the stained vitreous, at the same time replacing it with clear saline solution. This procedure can not only eliminate the clouded vision, but it can also give the ophthalmologist an opportunity to see into your eyes and evaluate the usefulness of laser treatment.

Is Aspirin a Preventive?

There is some thought today that aspirin in the correct daily dosage may help prevent retinopathy, and this theory is now being studied at the National Eye Institute in Maryland. Aspirin tends to reduce the rate at which blood platelets clump together. If retinopathy is the result of decreased oxygen flow to the retina because of an accelerated clumping effect typical in diabetes, then aspirin may allow the blood to reach the eyes more easily.

One aspirin tablet (5 grains) a day may be a good precaution. Until we know the drug's effects and the right dosage, we suggest you take aspirin every day as a possible preventive for both retinopathy and arteriosclerosis.

Caution: If you already have retinopathy and have a tendency toward leaking capillaries, then aspirin may be *harmful*. Do not take it unless your ophthalmologist recommends it, because its anticoagulating effect may increase your bleeding. Keep in mind that the blood is in a constant fight to keep a balance between clotting and bleeding.

Will Vitamin C Help?

Though vitamin C in combination with rutin was once widely prescribed for retinopathy, studies have shown that rutin isn't absorbed by the body at all, and the effectiveness of vitamin C as a way to strengthen the capillary walls is currently being hotly debated. In other words, nobody knows for sure whether it will help prevent retinopathy, or colds either for that matter. Our theory is, though, that it can't hurt to take about 500 mgs of C every day. The best that could happen is that it works; the worst is that it doesn't. Excess vitamin C is excreted in the urine. Remember, though, that large doses may interfere with urine-testing results (see page 127).

What About Magnesium?

A study comparing three groups of diabetics found the lowest amount of magnesium in those with the greatest degree of retinopathy. From this it has been theorized that supplements of magnesium salts may be beneficial. Again, we don't have the answer yet. Since magnesium can be found in such foods as meat, cereals and nuts, be sure you get enough of them.

My Vision Is Blurry. Is That Bad?

Not necessarily. Your vision can be affected simply by your current blood-sugar level. If the level is high or fluctuating, your sight may be fuzzy, out of focus. It will clear up when you're once more under good control, though it may take anywhere from a few days to a few weeks. Blurred vision is *expected* when your diabetes is first diagnosed and you are treated with insulin for the first time. After undergoing a week or two of insulin therapy and your blood sugar goes down to an acceptable level, you may find you cannot focus clearly. Don't panic. It will get better before long.

Probably the blurred vision occurs because, during the period of poor control and dehydration, the eyes gradually lost some of their fluid content as well as fluids from the rest of the body, altering their shape. In addition, the increased sugar content in the eyes' lenses may cause them to swell and alter their refraction of light. As both these factors swing back toward normal, you will notice the blurriness until you adjust once more.

By the way, be sure your sugar is in optimum control *before* you go to the ophthalmologist for new eyeglasses. If your sugar is high, your distance vision may be affected. If it is very low, your near vision may change. So new glasses that are fitted today may not be right for you tomorrow or next week. If you are a new diabetic, wait at least a month after you have been stabilized before going for a prescription.

What Causes Double Vision?

Very low blood-sugar levels can temporarily produce double vision. If the two images persist, however, it may be due to infarction of a nerve of the eye muscles and an uneven pull of the muscles. If an eye is pulled off-center unilaterally, you will see two images, a decidedly unpleasant phenomenon. But don't worry, it disappears spontaneously in just about every case within three or four weeks, and all you'll need is an eye patch until it does.

Do Diabetics Have More Cataracts?

Probably not. But, when they get them, the progression is more rapid. Cataracts include both the "snowflake" metabolic variety that occasionally occurs in juvenile diabetics and the "senile" kind that is part of the normal aging process.

Treatment for cataracts is the same for everyone, though for diabetics the doctors may decide on surgery at a slightly earlier stage of development in order to have an opportunity to examine the back of the retina.

With cataract surgery, as with any other kind of operation, it is very important to be under optimum control so that healing will be normal and infections more easily avoided.

You may consider a lens implant at the time of surgery. This will not interfere with laser treatment if you ever require it. Or you may prefer contact lenses or the thicker special glasses made for people who have had cataracts removed.

Are Contact Lenses Safe?

There is no reason you cannot wear contact lenses if the outer surfaces of your eyes are in healthy condition. Be sure, however, to go to a reputable ophthalmologist who has extensive experience in fitting contacts. You may choose hard or soft lenses which are taken out every day; or a new variety called semipermanent. These lenses are removed, examined and replaced by the eye doctor every three months.

Should I Worry About "Floaters"?

Floaters or "flying mice," as they have been dubbed, are little pieces of protein that you can see fleetingly as they float through the vitreous, the gel-like fluid within the eyeball. These are nothing to be concerned about. Lots of people have them, though diabetics seem to have them more often than others.

The Effect of Marijuana and Other Drugs

Marijuana lowers the pressure within the eyeball, so it is theoretically possible that it may encourage bleeding of the fragile capillaries on the retina. This is a good reason, along with a few others, not to use it. It encourages a desire for sweets among some people, which diabetics can't afford, and tends to alter the sense of time. You may forget to eat on time and have a serious insulin reaction.

Some medications, such as one used to lower cholesterol, also tend to decrease intraocular pressure and may be dangerous if you have retinopathy.

The Effects of Exercise

Regular vigorous exercise helps to prevent retinopathy and other diabetic complications. But, the story is quite different if you already have retinopathy. Now it's important *not* to raise your blood pressure, which can trigger more hemorrhaging of those tiny blood vessels in the backs of the eyes. Don't do anything strenuous without consulting your doctor.

Kidney Problems

Because your two kidneys, located just to either side of your spine, are intricate filters with the important job of eliminating waste products from the blood while holding on to certain vital proteins, it is very important that they continue to function smoothly. Kidney complications, however, can be one of the problems that beset long-time diabetics. This is because of a tendency for the walls or "basement membranes" of the kidneys' complex network of capillaries to thicken and, at the same time, become too porous. These incredibly complicated filters then allow a loss of proteins—albumin and globulin—into the urine. Further progression can result in uremia and kidney failure, which can only be treated by dialysis or kidney transplants.

Other factors that can lead to kidney complications are high blood pressure and urinary infections, problems diabetics are prone to have. Pressure control is important, and so is the early and vigorous treatment of infections.

And, as always, keep your diabetes under good control. There is solid evidence that kidney damage can be prevented or at least lessened by strict control, and other indications that it might even be somewhat reversible.

Neuropathy

Neuropathy, probably the most common as well as the strangest of all the possible diabetic complications, affects nerve function and isn't very well understood even today.

Its symptoms can be mild and simply an annoyance, or they can make life pretty miserable. The only good thing about neuropathy is that its weird effects often disappear or improve dramatically after a while. This can take from a couple of months to a couple of years.

Because neuropathy is nerve damage that both interferes with the ability of the nerves to conduct messages and at times actually alters them, sometimes it results in outright severe pain, sometimes in tingling, a pins-and-needles sensation, burning, itching or simply numbness. Occasionally there will be pain and numbness at the same time. These symptoms, which can show up in many parts of the body, come and go unpredictably, though for most people they tend to be decidedly worse at night. And they often confound the medical experts, who may diagnose them as something else.

Nobody knows just why neuropathy happens, but recent research indicates that the "sorbitol pathway" may be at the bottom of it. When sugar persistently circulates at high levels in the body tissues, certain enzymes turn the glucose into fructose, then into sorbitol. Sorbitol, a sugar that cannot return to its previous incarnations as glucose and fructose, causes damage to the nerves so they are unable to carry on their normal metabolism and consequently their normal function. (Sorbital taken by mouth, however, does not affect the nerves.)

Where Neuropathy Strikes

Neuropathy most often affects the legs and feet, where it gives you pain or tingling, or the odd impression of walking on sand or pebbles. Often there's a *lack* of sensation, so it feels as if you are walking on wood or even on pillows or clouds. Some people say it feels as if their feet do not belong to them. Others have pain and lack of sensation at the very same time and some become extraordinarily sensitive to touch so that even the weight of sheets is a torment. The pain may be constant or intermittent, usually becoming much more troublesome at night. Often it occurs *only* at night, disappearing when the sun comes up. Cold, wet weather seems to aggravate it.

If you haven't much feeling in your feet, you will now have to be especially careful not to injure them without realizing it, and to keep an eye out for infections you can't feel. See Chapter 13 for a complete discussion of foot care. care.

If you have neuropathic pain, take comfort in the fact that it may get better in a few months. In fact, some specialists say the worse the pain, the faster it goes away, leaving some numbness in its place. Meantime, you may need painkillers or tranquilizers to help you sleep. Some physicians prescribe an antidepressant with a mood elevator so that narcotics can be avoided in the quest for a good night's sleep. This can be quite effective. Others prescribe Dilantin, which I don't recommend because, in my experience, it usually doesn't work and it decreases whatever insulin secretion you have, interfering with glucose metabolism if you are on oral agents or diet alone.

Other Neuropathic Haunts

Though the feet are neuropathy's favorite targets, it can affect other parts of you too. Occasionally people find their hands become somewhat insensitive, almost as if they are wearing gloves, or the muscles of the hands diminish in size. Diabetics also sometimes develop a condition called Dupuytren's contracture. The tendons of the palm of the hand become thickened and shortened, hindering mobility. Surgery can correct these "frozen" hands.

Occasionally neuropathy affects the muscles of the eyes, causing double vision and perhaps sharp pain. The prognosis is usually excellent for double vision, with complete recovery within about six weeks.

The gastrointestinal tract is another part of the body that may be affected by this strange nerve damage peculiar to diabetes. The esophagus and stomach, as well as the intestines, may not contract with their usual vigor, with the result that they don't empty efficiently. The delay may affect your diabetic control by delaying the absorption of the food. Or it may cause bloating or perhaps nausea.

Some people with intestinal neuropathy find they develop diarrhea at unpredictable moments (most often at night). Or they become severely constipated. About half of those with diabetic diarrhea respond nicely to antibiotics that work on the intestinal bacteria. Other people get good results from antidiarrhea medications such as Lomotil or codeine. The constipation usually responds to laxatives or stool softeners. Drugs such as Metoclopramide to stimulate smooth muscle tissue may be helpful as well. Keep in mind that fatigue and stress have a poor effect on bowel problems.

The bladder may also be affected by this strange villain if the nerve damage interferes with its ability to contract, or with its owner's ability to sense when it is full and needs emptying. The urine may back up into the kidneys or the bladder may not empty completely, providing a happy home for bacteria and infections.

Urinary Problems

Because constant urinary infections that may hang on stubbornly can eventually lead to serious kidney disfunction, all diabetics must be sure to watch closely for them.

If you have any reason to believe you have an infection, see your doctor immediately, be certain you are given the proper tests to determine the right drugs to combat it, and that you stay on the drugs until the infection is totally destroyed. If you have a tendency to get infections, your doctor should check for infection by examining the urine under a microscope at every examination (at least every three months) whether or not you have symptoms.

If you notice you are not urinating very often and, when you do, you produce a less-than-expected amount, discuss this with your doctor, who may suggest that you urinate every few hours on schedule rather than wait for the urge, or may prescribe drugs to stimulate urination.

Neuropathic Ulcers

Because neuropathy often causes a lack of feeling on the bottoms of the feet, it's possible to develop sores, usually at pressure points, that you are unaware of. This causes calluses which then put more pressure on the area. Eventually, unnoticed, a neuropathic ulcer may form beneath the calluses, becoming infected and leading to serious trouble if it is unchecked.

See Chapter 13 for advice on avoiding this kind of foot problem before it starts. Once an ulcer develops, it must be treated immediately and vigorously if you don't want to be in for a long siege. The infection must be drained and a course of antibiotics begun *promptly*. Then the pressure must be relieved, either by staying off your feet or by special wedges or inner soles in your shoes.

Because of the potential seriousness of an ulcer, your feet should be examined constantly by you and periodically by both your doctor and your podiatrist.

The Rarer Neuropathies

A few other neuropathic effects include:

- Orthostatic hypotension, which is temporary low pressure occurring when you stand up suddenly or raise your head. This makes you dizzy and sometimes unsteady on your feet for a few moments. Medication can help, along with support panty hose to help constrict the blood vessels in the legs.
- Abnormal sweating may be a form of neuropathy, especially when it appears on the face (or *half* the face) after eating.
- "Dry foot," when the feet don't produce sweat and so tend to dry out and crack. Or the opposite, feet that are particularly sweaty.
- Radicular pain, a sharp abdominal pain, which usually recedes after a while.
- Charcot's joint, a relatively rare phenomenon where the small bones in the joints of the feet become misaligned, and the foot tends to become flatter and wider; and "foot drop" when certain muscles weaken. Braces or temporary casts are often part of the therapy.
- Sexual impotence after many years of diabetes, and retrograde ejaculation, which means the semen flows back into the bladder rather than out of the penis. See Chapter 15.

What's the Outlook for Neuropathy?

Because not too much is known about what actually causes neuropathy, not much is known about what to do about it either. In some cases, medication can be helpful. In others, the symptoms disappear as mysteriously as they came, and most usually go away eventually or markedly improve.

In the early stages, 50 to 100 mgs of vitamin B_1 taken

daily can be effective. If it isn't, try B$_{12}$ injections up to 20 units. If you wish you can inject this along with your insulin. Experimental work is now underway to test the effectiveness of a drug called Myonisotol in increasing nerve conduction. This is a substance found in the nerve coverings, and also in cantaloupes and peanuts. On the chance this natural form may help you, test it out by eating a quarter of a cantaloupe in place of other vitamin C fruits in the morning and perhaps another quarter for dessert after dinner instead of another fruit or ice cream. Peanuts are probably too laden with calories for you, but if you are thin, you could try them out. Remember to count their carbohydrate value into your meal allotments.

If your neuropathy causes pain, you and your doctor will have to come up with medication that works for you, taking care that, in your eagerness to dull the discomfort, you don't become dependent on the drugs. This can become more of a problem than the discomfort.

Also under investigation is a sorbitol-blocking drug that may hold some answers.

And let's not forget *control*. Obviously, good control may help you avoid the neuropathies in the first place. And it is quite possible it can prevent further progress of problems you already have.

Note: if you have been in poor control for a long time, have developed neuropathy, and now set forth on the path to good control, you may find that any neuropathic discomforts are aggravated at first. This may tempt you to revert to your old bad habits. But hold on. If you stay with it, you will soon feel better.

Diabetes and Your Teeth

No doubt you'd like to keep a complete set of your very own teeth forever—nobody looks forward to dropping his teeth into a glass every night. If so, you are going to have to take extraordinarily good care of them, because you are more susceptible than most people to gum disease, the major cause of tooth loss. That is another result of the effect of diabetes on the body's myriads of tiny capillaries. The thickened walls of the little blood vessels make oxygen-vs.-waste exchange less efficient. And you are then more likely to develop infections that are difficult to get rid of. If your diabetes is poorly controlled, your white blood cells, whose job it is to fight off bacteria, are less effective in their battle against infection, causing it to become more severe and harder to heal.

Brushing and Flossing

What this means is that you must practice excellent dental hygiene so you won't run into these problems. Using a soft toothbrush (hard ones can scratch the gums), brush your teeth carefully after every meal. Don't scrub, but use downward strokes.

Then *every night* before going to bed and just after you have brushed your teeth, take some unwaxed dental floss and floss out the plaque that accumulates around each tooth under the gumline in places that the tooth brush doesn't reach. Gently, gently! Ask your dentist or dental hygienist to give you a lesson in the proper way to do this: Wind the ends of the floss around your two forefingers, then *gently* pull the taut center section between two teeth. Do not snap it in because you must be careful not to injure your gums. Then, first to the left, then to the right, curving the floss into a U-shape, gently dislodge the plaque from around the gumline of each tooth. When you have done this between all your teeth, rinse out your mouth.

If you are not sure you have done a good job with the

flossing, you can buy some special vegetable dye that will show you the places you have missed. It is made for this purpose.

Gum massage is another useful preventive measure because it improves the circulation. After each brushing, take your fingers and gently but firmly give your gums a good rub. Better yet, use a special gum massager with a rubber tip. And check out your dentist's opinion of a water-jet gadget that is designed to get rid of the debris caught in and around your teeth that isn't dislodged by brushing.

See your dentist *at least* every four to six months, both for a good cleaning—it's important that hardened plaque or tartar is removed that often—and to check out your gums. If you have developed periodontal disease, immediate treatment is what you need. Be sure your dentist is thoroughly knowledgable about gum disease, diabetes and current methods of treatment.

More Tooth Tips

• Before you have any dental work done, *including cleaning*, which frequently results in injured gums, you should be "covered" by antibiotics. That means, because you are susceptible to infections, all preventive measures should be taken automatically. You should have three days of antibiotic treatment—the day before, the day of, and the day after the dental work.

• Some drugs, such as Dilantin, can have an adverse effect on your gums.

• If you have periodontal work done on your gums, that doesn't mean you can now forget the flossing and the massage. The problems will return if you don't work hard to prevent them.

• Be sure to get your diabetes under excellent control

before having any periodontal surgery, so you will have the best chance of fast healing.

• If, because of periodontal work or extractions, you must eat soft or liquid foods for a while, remember that you must still abide by a proper diabetic diet. Liquids are fine, but they do contain calories and perhaps sugar and must be accounted for just as if they were solid foods. If you are confused about substitutions (see Chapter 4), work it out with your doctor or a dietician *before* you get into trouble.

Diabetes and Your Skin

For all the same reasons that you tend to get infections more easily than people with normal blood sugar, and have a harder time fighting them off, youy may discover you have skin problems more often too. If you do, look to your control. Though the blame for these may be shared by microvascular changes and sluggish white cells that aren't so quick to attack bacteria and other invaders, remember that high sugar is the real villain, and that skin infections are often the direct result of poorly controlled diabetes. In fact, boils, styes, inflammation around the nails, and other eruptions are often the clue that makes a physician suspect you have diabetes in the first place. Poor control also causes dry, itchy skin, which you may scratch and irritate, issuing an invitation to an invasion of bacteria.

Poor control promotes the appearance of fungus or yeast infections of the vagina in women, of the groin in men, and sometimes of the anus regardless of your gender. Your doctor can prescribe effective medication. Your job is to use it faithfully and get yourself back in good condition. Fungi also make homes in armpits, between fingers and toes, around the nails, and other moist places.

Spots and Other Problems

Fairly common among long-term diabetics is "spotted leg syndrome" or "skin spots." These little brown pock-marks that start out looking like reddish bruises usually appear on the shins where tiny end capillaries have shut down. They don't hurt and they don't get worse, though we know of no way to get rid of them.

A skin condition called "necrobiosis lipoidica diabeticorum" (NLD) is the special province of diabetics and it, too, is worrisome chiefly for cosmetic reasons. Necrobiosis is the appearance, frequently on the lower legs, of patches of reddish-brown lesions. These become areas of tight, shiny skin like glazed parchment paper that is indented because of a loss of subcutaneous fat just beneath it. Sometimes they are itchy or even painful; or they may crack. The spots are often discolored, but they tend to fade with time, although this may take a few years. Some doctors have successfully treated NLD with fine-needle injections of cortisone, though usually no treatment is needed except to prevent injury or infection.

Ulcers, which start out as a skin problem, soon become more than that if the infection deepens and extends into the surrounding tissue. If you discover even the smallest indication of infection, especially on your legs or feet, call your doctor immediately. Prompt treatment to avert big trouble is what you need.

Insulin Atrophy and Hypertrophy

A cosmetic problem called lipodystrophy (insulin atrophy and hypertrophy) is, happily, becoming much less common among diabetics today as purer insulins are developed. Insulin atrophy, which appears in areas where insulin injections are given frequently, is a loss of fatty tissue just below the skin, causing large depressions that look scooped out. This can make a person—and usually this happens to young women—most unhappy, but generally the areas eventually fill in again and disappear.

Sometimes insulin injections promote an abnormal buildup of fat, and so you have lumps instead of hollows, or occasionally both. This is called insulin hypertrophy.

If this happens to you, try not to inject into identical sites continually. Rotate your shots so you don't hit the same place more than once a month. Keep a record of your sites to help you do this. Another way to treat scooped-out areas is to inject them continuously with the hope that hypertrophy will be induced and fill in the hallows.

With the new monocomponent insulins, your problems may disappear with no treatment at all. Because many contaminants have been removed, they are much less likely to cause adverse responses.

Diabetic blisters (bullosa diabeticorum) are painless raised areas that look like burn blisters. These are quite rare and happen to people whose diabetes is out of control. To get rid of them, attend to your blood sugar. They will disappear in a few weeks.

Small, hard pealike bumps with red halos and an itch are another sign of lack of diabetic control and will disappear when you are in better shape. This condition is called eruptive xanthomatosis.

Everyday Skin Care

If you allow your skin to become dry and chapped—and dry skin is a characteristic of diabetics (in fact, the skin becomes dehydrated where your control is poor)—you will not only be inviting bacteria, but you will lower the skin's ability to serve as a barrier to the loss of body water. Don't take too many baths, especially in cold weather. Don't wash too often with soap, or use disinfectants or solvents. Try super-fatted soaps. Wear gloves and scarves and warm socks or stockings when you're out in the cold. Invest in a home humidifier.

To add moisture to your skin and protect it, soak (your whole body or just the dry area) in warm water for several minutes, pat off the excess water, then apply a greasy ointment like petroleum jelly or lanolin, or a good dry-skin cream or lotion. For everyday use, try a product that contains urea.

If you use bath oil, pour the oil in the tub *after* you have soaked yourself for a while. In this way, your skin will first absorb some water which the oil will help to retain. If you put the oil in the water before you have absorbed some moisture into your skin, it will form a barrier to that moisture.

The same principle applies to moisturizing lotion or cream whose purpose is to seal water in. Wet your skin and pat it almost dry before applying the moisturizer.

TWELVE

Rules
for Sick Days

Just like everybody else, you are going to get sick occasionally. But, unlike everybody else, you will discover your life promptly becomes much more complicated simply because you are a diabetic with an infection. Infections can be more difficult to get rid of and often more severe for you because your defenses may not be the best. Besides, with most illnesses your insulin requirements will rise, sometimes quite dramatically.

All this means that control may be hard to maintain during an illness, so now your objective is not only to recover from the illness but also to avoid acidosis and a trip to the hospital.

If you are on diet alone or diet plus oral agents, remember you are not immune to high blood sugars, acetone and acidosis when you are sick. You may need temporary shots of insulin to get through, so never neglect your urine tests. Instead of one a day, increase them to thee or four. If you normally take insulin, your chief occupation now will be testing your urine or blood and adjusting your dose. You will undoubtedly need more insulin, maybe two or three times more than usual.

When you are sick, you must live by the rules:

RULE 1: Stay in close touch with your doctor. If you feel your physician doesn't like to be bothered by frequent (not excessive) phone calls or is not providing the guidance you need, find another one. Check with the American Diabetic Association or Juvenile Diabetes Foundation in your area for a recommendation. The doctor is the person who must make the medical decisions, some major, some minor, when you are sick. Remember the telephone is your friend. If you see a problem evolving during the day, however, call early. Any doctor would rather hear from you at 6 or 10 P.M. than 2 A.M., but better 2 A.M. than not at all if you are in bad shape.

RULE 2: When you are sick, *check your blood or urine at least four times a day,* before each meal and at bedtime. If you are seriously ill, check it every *two* hours. Just as you are never too tired to breathe, you are *never* too tired or sick or weak to test yourself. You must know where your **blood sugar stands** because the test will tell you what to do next.

RULE 3: When blood sugar is high, the diabetic who takes insulin must compensate with extra insulin, the fast-acting (Regular) variety. Your doctor will tell you how much to take. A common recommendation is 20 percent of the units of your normal daily Intermediate-acting dose, taken every two to four hours.

To figure that out, divide the units of your usual dose by 5 to get 1/5 or 20 percent. For example, 60 units divided by 5 = 12 units. So, if you normally take 60 units of NPH or Lente every morning, now you will continue to take that amount. In addition, test your blood or urine every two to four hours as long as your high sugar persists, and take 12 more units of Regular if the sugar level continues to be high.

When you get a high sugar reading, *always test for acetone*. The presence of acetone *along with* high sugar means you need extra insulin quickly. Now you may require even *more* extra Regular insulin every two hours until the sugar comes down, according to your doctor's instructions. This is vital if you want to avoid acidosis.

If your sugar is negative and your acetone is positive, never take extra insulin. Take only your usual dose. A reading of low sugar with high acetone means the acetone has not been entirely washed out of the body (it may remain for about 24 hours after your sugar has been regulated back to normal); or that your body lacks its primary fuel—sugar—and is burning fat, one of the end products of which is acetone. You now need carbohydrate—juice, bread, cereal, milk, etc.—to avoid an insulin reaction and to give your body its normal fuel. Check with your doctor.

After you have lowered your blood sugar with increased insulin, it may be wise to set your alarm clock for 3 A.M. Check your blood sugar and eat something if it is negative.

Sickness is rarely a major diabetic problem for a person controlled only by diet, but it can be. Even you can develop acidosis if you allow high sugars to persist without taking action. Call your doctor if you have high sugars for more than 24 hours. You may require temporary insulin because the stress of illness can raise your insulin requirement far beyond the ability of your pancreas to produce it.

When you take oral agents, your insulin needs will rise because of the additional release of glucose from the liver during an infection. The result may be that the amount of insulin produced by your own pancreas with the help of the oral agent won't be enough to cover the sugar and prevent the end result of acidosis. Your doctor must make the decision as to whether you should take more of the oral agent until your blood sugar drops, or whether you will need insulin injections temporarily. When you have reached your maximum dosage of oral hypoglycemic agents, taking an additional amount is useless because no more insulin can be coaxed out of your islet cells. If you continue to spill sugar and produce acetone, you will be instructed to use insulin—either alone or as a supplement to the pills—until your glucose levels are normal once more. Call your doctor, who will probably prescribe five to ten units of quick-acting insulin every two hours.

RULE 4: Always keep Regular insulin on hand, whether or not you normally use it. This fast-acting insulin is what you will need to counteract high sugar quickly.

RULE 5: *Never* omit your daily insulin, *even if you are eating less than usual or not at all*. Your diabetes does not disappear just because you can't eat, and your liver continues to manufacture glucose, perhaps much more than usual.

If your sugar tests are *positive*, take your normal dose. Then consult with your doctor about an extra amount.

If your sugar is *negative* but you cannot eat, take *half* your usual dose.

Continue to test throughout the day. Don't wait till tomorrow, hoping you'll wake up cured. You may wake up in the hospital instead.

If you are on oral agents, never omit your pills, even when you cannot eat much, because you must still overcome your raised blood-sugar level.

RULE 6. Try to eat. Even if you are not hungry or you are nauseated, you can usually find something that will go down and stay there. To prevent acidosis, you need at least 50 to 60 grams of carbohydrate a day. If you can't stick to your usual diet plan, switch over to food that goes down most easily and eat it in smaller amounts spaced through the day. If you can't eat normal meals, now is the time for you to eat carbohydrates, so that you get sufficient fuel.

Try toast, crackers, soups, eggs, cottage cheese, yogurt, juices, custard, ice cream. Perhaps grapefruit, eggnog, cereal. Your goal should be 10 grams of carbohydrate an hour.

If liquids are all you can manage, drink your food, remembering that you must have sufficient carbohydrate as well as salt to replace the salt lost by excessive urination. Clear soup, salty broth, tea with sugar, juice, milk, regular (not diet) ginger ale or cola to give you the carbohydrate you need may appeal to you. Take some about every half hour in small amounts.

If you can't eat or drink at all, inform your doctor immediately.

Easy-to-Eat Foods*

Applesauce	Jams or jellies, regular
Bread	Jello, regular
Broth, bouillon	Popsicle
Cereal	Postum
Coffee	Sherbet
Cottage cheese	Soft drinks, regular
Crackers	Soups
Custard	Sugar
Egg	Tapioca
Eggnog	Tea
Fruit juices	Tomato juice
Ice Cream	Vegetable cocktail
Ice Milk	Yogurt

* © 1979 by American Diabetes Association. Reprinted from *Diabetes Forecast* with permission.

RULE 7: Try to control vomiting as quickly as possible. Three ounces of regular ginger ale every hour often acts as an antiemetic and provides the needed carbohydrate too. If that doesn't banish the nausea, your doctor can prescribe a suppository or give you an antinausea injection. Tigan suppositories (200 mgs for adults or 100 mg for children who weigh less than 30 pounds) every eight hours, or Compazine suppositories (up to 25 mg for adults, 5 mgs for older children, 2.5 mgs for young children) every eight hours are usually effective.

If you can't eat or drink at all or you are continuing to vomit, call your doctor *immediately*. You may need intravenous infusions of saline solution and/or glucose.

Continue to take your usual insulin or oral agent, plus Regular insulin every two hours if your sugar is high.

RULE 8: Control diarrhea as quickly as possible, too, because it can cause the loss of valuable fluids and carbohydrates. Usually a drug such as Lomotil works well, but if you have diarrhea and nausea at the same time, you won't be able to keep it down nor can you use suppositories! An intramuscular injection of Compazine, which your doctor can prescribe, may be the solution. *Call the doctor* for instructions.

RULE 9: There is no need to stay in bed, but it's important to rest as much as possible. Do not exercise. If you are very sick, it would be advisable to have someone to take care of you.

RULE 10: If you are taking antibiotics, you will have an increased tendency to get fungal infections—vaginitis, rectal itching, skin infections. When you are given an antibiotic, you should also be given lactobacillus, perhaps a preparation called BACID. Plain yogurt eaten in place of fruit or bread may help prevent an overgrowth of the fungi.

RULE 11: Check all medication for sugar. Many cold medicines as well as other drugs are loaded with it and can throw your control off in a hurry. Sudafed and Triaminic syrups, for example, contain 3½ grams of carbohydrate per teaspoon. If you take three teaspoons a day for a cold, you are adding 10½ grams of unwanted simple sugar to your bloodstream. Robitussin cough syrup contains 2.8 grams per teaspoon, or 11.2 extra grams if you take the recommended 4 teaspoons a day. Other cold medicines have similar carbohydrate contents.

You certainly should not add this much sugar to your body at a time when you are already under the stress of infection and your glucose tolerance is disturbed because of the release of cortisone from your adrenal glands. It is possible, however, to get medications without sugar. Cough medicines that are sugar-free include Cidicol, Dimetapp Elixir, Cerose, Cerose DM, and Tussar SF.

RULE 12: *Keep a careful record* of all your test results, insulin intake, food and drink. Omit nothing. Write this information down so that you can refer to it when you discuss your situation with your doctor. Include comments on how you feel, whether you are vomiting, have diarrhea, a temperature, etc., each time you record your test results.

Injuries and Surgery

Both surgery and physical injuries are an assault on your diabetic control because they stimulate the body's defense mechanism to pour out cortisone and adrenaline which increase your blood sugar. So you must double your efforts at these times to maintain good control, making frequent tests and perhaps taking additional insulin.

If you are in good control, you'll have no special problems recovering from surgery and will heal just about as quickly as anyone else. When you expect surgery, bring your sugar into the normal range and keep it there, if you can. Otherwise, you may find that acidosis lurks just around the corner and that you'll heal with difficulty. The best-known anabolic (tissue-building) agent is insulin.

Of course, your doctor is in charge when you are in the hospital and will make adjustments in your medication to regulate your sugar both during the operative procedure and postoperatively. Your insulin will be increased, or, if you don't normally take it, you may have to go the insulin route temporarily until you are stable once more.

Even when you are in the hospital, the rules still apply. "They gave it to me" is no excuse for eating so much carbohydrate that your blood sugar will go sky high. If you are suffering from an infection or the stress of surgery, your blood sugar will tend to run high anyway—don't make it worse by eating the wrong foods. See page 38 in the diet chapter.

Beware Drug Interactions

If you have an illness that requires you take a drug, be sure your doctor remembers you are a diabetic. If you go to a specialist who does not know your history, give out the information immediately. Not only does your diabetes affect your illness, but the drugs prescribed may affect your diabetes.

For example, oral cortisone raises insulin requirements. Diabetics on insulin may need a higher dose, and those on diet or oral agents may need to take insulin while taking cortisone. People often do not know that Prednisone or Medrol or Decamethasone are cortisone drugs.

Dilantin is a major drug used for epilepsy or convulsive disorders. It has the ability to inhibit insulin release, so even people with borderline diabetes can be thrown out of control when they use this drug. Even though it is sometimes prescribed for diabetic neuropathy, it can be dangerous. See pages 150, 171.

Inderal, a drug commonly prescribed for angina, headaches and hypertension, can mask an insulin reaction as mentioned in Chapter 9. When blood sugar is low, the adrenal glands secrete adrenaline which releases sugar from the liver. A rapid heart beat, sweating, and other symptoms generally alert you to the fact that you are becoming hypoglycemic, but Inderal blocks this effect so that you may not be aware of your precarious situation. Certain other drugs affect the action of the oral agents, too, enhancing their effectiveness and sometimes producing hypoglycemic reactions. To repeat the list, these include: Coumadin, Butazoladine, Benemid, Dilantin, Atromid S, sulfonamides, mood ameliorators and a number of other medications.

The action of drugs such as barbiturates, sedatives and hypnotics can be greatly prolonged when they are taken together with oral agents. In addition, the effect of the oral agents may be prolonged as well. Don't take any chances. Before you take a new drug, be sure to check out its effect on your diabetes.

THIRTEEN

Watching Your Feet

WHEN you are a diabetic, you hear a lot about taking good care of your feet. It may seem like a minor issue, but it's extremely important that you follow all the rules about foot care if you want to avoid some most unpleasant problems in the future. Any injuries or infections of the feet and ankles and even lower legs are potentially very dangerous to the diabetic. They can lead to serious complications that can be treated only by drastic surgery which you don't even want to think about. The most common reason for the amputation of feet and legs is long-term diabetes, so the big word now is *prevention*. Don't let anything get started. And if it should, go *immediately* to your doctor.

A diabetic, especially if control has been poor for a number of years, tends to have poor circulation in the legs and feet. This is particularly true for older people. The small arteries become narrower and cannot carry the optimum amounts of blood, oxygen and infection-fighting white cells to these extremities. That makes diabetics particularly susceptible to injuries and infections such as carbuncles, boils and athlete's foot, which can become serious problems *very* quickly. It also tends to produce dry skin that cracks more easily.

Sometimes the nerve endings, as well as the circulation, are affected. Diabetics often have neuropathy—damage to the small sensory nerves—and that means you may not have the feeling in your feet that you once had. You can cut yourself, wear shoes that rub, step on sharp objects or burn yourself and never realize it. You can get athlete's foot or other infections without knowing it. Meanwhile, the wound or infection can rapidly turn into a major problem. For a nondiabetic a little cut, a rub, a blister, a fungus, may be only an annoyance. For a diabetic, it could be the start of deep trouble, so you can't let it go, even for a few days.

That's why, though you may find it a nuisance, you must consciously pay attention to your feet every single day. Actually it's easy and takes only a few minutes, and it wouldn't be a bad idea if everyone did the same thing. Feet are rarely anyone's favorite part of the body and are usually totally ignored and maltreated until they start causing some discomfort. But you can't afford to ignore yours—you *must* head off any problems before they begin if you possibly can.

You have to abide by a list of simple rules of hygiene, remember a number of things you should and should not do, make periodic appointments with a reputable podiatrist and, most important, waste no time in checking with your podiatrist and/or your doctor if you notice the slightest sign of a problem, even a small discoloration. Never assume that whatever it is will just clear up on its own. It might, but it might not. Never treat your feet yourself except under the direction of your doctor. Never assume anything is too minor to worry about. Always remember you must not wait until you feel pain to become concerned—

you may not feel a thing and yet be brewing serious problems. Don't take any chances.

Everyday Foot Care

Washing: Wash your feet every day. Yes, every day. They must be kept clean. This does not mean soaking them, not a wise practice for diabetics. In fact, it is dangerous and actually encourages infection by softening the skin so much that it may break easily and provide a home for bacteria and fungi.

Because your skin is probably very dry, use a nonalkaline soap. (If you're not sure which brands are nonalkaline, ask your druggist for one. It will not require a prescription.) Be especially careful to avoid deodorant soaps, which are particularly drying.

Be sure the water is only warm (below 92° F.), *never* hot.

Red Flag! If you have a loss of pain perception, common in many diabetics, you may not notice the water is too hot if you carelessly dip your feet in without testing it first. Don't test with your toe. Use your hand or your elbow. Or use a thermometer. One thing you must not have is burned feet.

Now take a soft towel and carefully dry your feet. Do not rub between your toes, because the skin here is thin and delicate, but pat off the moisture to avoid irritation.

Examining: This is the moment to take a close look at every square millimeter of your feet and lower legs. Every day. If your eyesight isn't good or you have trouble bending over that far, enlist someone else to do this. We'll say it again: If you see any broken skin, peeling, redness, irritation, bruises, swelling, *anything* that even vaguely strikes you as unusual, don't treat it yourself and don't waste a moment. Go immediately to your podiatrist or physician.

By the way, every diabetic should have a good podiatrist, a specialist in foot care. Podiatrists are frequently much more knowledgeable about foot and leg problems than doctors.

Skin Care: After you have examined your feet closely, use some baby powder between your toes. Then gently rub a skin-softening lotion or cream on your feet and legs to counteract the dryness, except between your toes where you do not want moisture. Avoid any lotions that contain medication or alcohol.

Pedicures

For most diabetics, it is an excellent idea to go to a podiatrist as often as necessary to have your toenails trimmed. It is much better than doing it yourself. That's because a small slip of the scissors can be the start of trouble. Especially if your toenails are thick—as they often are in older people—it is best for an expert to do the job. Besides, your visit will be an opportunity for this expert to check out your feet to be sure all is well. You will have a chance to ask questions and get advice, eliminating vague worries from your mind and forestalling any ill-advised self-treatment.

If you are going to do the pedicuring yourself at any time, keep the following rules in mind. Use manicuring scissors with blunt rounded tips, the kind used for cutting babies' nails. Cut your nails after a bath so they will be soft. Trim them *straight across,* even with the ends of your toes. If they are too long, you will have pressure on the nail bed; if they are too short, they will not protect your toes as they are intended to do and may expose the fragile skin beneath them.

Never cut cuticles or skin. Don't cut in at the corners,

because you will not only be in danger of cutting into the skin but you will also invite ingrown toenails. Don't use a nail file to keep your toenails in shape because you may unwittingly file your skin and irritate it. But you should use an emery board with a light touch to smooth down any rough edges.

If someone else does this job for you, be sure that person knows how to do it the right way. Give him/her this chapter to read.

Even More Advice

Now you may be thinking that all these rules about your feet are excessive, but we are going to add more anyway. If you want to stay in good shape, with two strong healthy feet holding you up for the rest of your life, don't skip to the next chapter but keep reading.

Check Out Your Footwear

Change your socks every day, more often if they get wet or your feet sweat a lot. If they don't fit perfectly, give them away. Your socks must not be too large or too small. They must not form wrinkles under your shoes. They must not have holes. Stretch socks or hosiery are not a good idea for you because they may restrict circulation or put pressure on your toes. Never wear socks or stockings with elasticized tops for the same reason. Furthermore, garters are out. Cotton or wool socks are the best choices because they are more absorbent that the synthetic fibers.

Never, never wear shoes that don't fit perfectly and comfortably. Each foot has 26 bones and 78 joints that must be well treated. Be sure there is enough room to accommodate all your toes in their natural positions, and that the heel is snug enough not to slide up and down. Buy shoes in the afternoon when your feet are the largest, and always have your feet measured standing, not sitting. Feet tend to get larger as you get older, so do not assume you wear the same size without checking.

If your sensory perception is not too good, you may not feel rubbing, so be sure to watch for it every time you take off your shoes and during your daily ablutions. Don't wear open toes—closed toes give much more protection. Break in new shoes gradually by wearing them around the house and then on short jaunts.

Get in the habit of feeling the insides of your shoes before you put them on, to be sure there aren't any protruding nails, bumps or rough spots that may be hazards.

If you can't find shoes that fit right, consult with your podiatrist who may have a solution for you.

Going barefoot, even in the house, is not for diabetics. The minute you step out of bed in the morning, put on a pair of slippers or shoes. Wear swim shoes or sneakers on the beach. Don't take a chance on stubbing your toe, getting a splinter, stepping on a piece of glass or a sharp shell, burning your feet on hot sand or cement.

Some More Important Don'ts

• Don't use medications or chemicals on your feet unless prescribed by your doctor (and be sure the doctor remembers you are diabetic); this includes over-the-counter foot remedies. Powerful medications, such as iodine, or medicated materials such as corn plasters, can destroy tissue or cause burns to delicate skin. A good rule is: If you can't put it on your face, don't put it on your feet. Tinted medicines, mercurochrome, for example, are taboo too because they can camouflage inflammation.

• Don't try bathroom surgery with scissors, razors or

even pumice stones or corn pads. If you develop a corn or a callus—which you shouldn't because you've thrown out your ill-fitting shoes—leave it alone! Let your podiatrist treat it. If you have poor weight distribution, which may be causing the corns or calluses, he may make a special mold for you to wear in your shoe to correct the problem.

• Don't use heat on your feet. Never put your feet in hot water. Remember to test the bath water with your hand or elbow. Stay out of saunas, steam rooms, whirlpool baths—most of them are too hot for your feet. Apply lots of sunscreen lotion when you are out in the sun—don't let them get sunburned. *Never* use hot-water bottles or heating pads.

• Don't let your feet get too chilled, either. Because your blood vessels are probably narrower and more constricted when you have diabetes, its easier for you to get frostbite. Invest in warm (but smooth) socks and roomy boots for cold weather. But don't wear boots indoors all day, because they can impede your circulation and, because they are warm, make your feet sweat and become susceptible to bacteria.

• Don't use adhesive tape. It can irritate the skin or even pull some skin away when you take it off. Instead, use the newer lightweight tapes.

• Don't smoke. Just one cigarette will constrict your peripheral blood vessels to an astonishing degree. Since yours are probably already narrower than normal, smoking will only compound the situation.

• That is a lot of nevers and don'ts, but all must be heeded.

Get Enough Exercise .

You need some kind of exercise every day because it will improve your circulation and encourage collateral vascular development. When your feet and the rest of you are in good condition, there is no exercise you can't do—from tennis to running to ice hockey. Nonathletes can move their blood around most efficiently by swimming or walking briskly at least a half hour every day.

Caution: if you have a foot or lower leg injury or infection, this is not the time for exercise. Even if it doesn't hurt, walking on injuries can damage them further.

FOURTEEN

Pregnancy Problems

C AN I have a baby? Will I have problems conceiving? Will the baby be normal? How risky is pregnancy for me? How will it affect my diabetes? Will the baby be diabetic? These are questions of immense importance to young women with diabetes. Happily, the answers today are astonishingly positive. Not many years ago, a diabetic woman conceived with difficulty and embarked on a hazardous trip when she became pregnant, with a good chance of losing her baby on the way and endangering her own health.

But today, the vast majority of diabetic women can have healthy babies, with only a slightly higher than normal statistical chance of spontaneous abortion, congenital anomalies and stillbirths, even in the presence of some serious diabetic complications. According to the Joslin Clinic, the fetal survival rate of diabetic pregnancies is now about 97 percent, while the rate for nondiabetics is 98 or 99 percent. That is a remarkably small difference. And maternal deaths today are almost nonexistent. Managing a diabetic pregnancy, however, requires excellent medical care, as well as complete cooperation on your part. This venture demands total dedication and motivation, hard work, time and attention. Besides, a diabetic pregnancy can be expensive. You may need the expert medical care of a whole team of specialists, many office visits, perhaps a number of hospitalizations, sophisticated laboratory tests, possibly a cesarean delivery.

For a happy outcome to a diabetic pregnancy, excellent blood-sugar control is the key. This is not so easy for an insulin-dependent woman, though it can definitely be achieved if you work at it. If you are controlled by diet alone, it is all much simpler. You may get along well simply by watching what you eat, paying strict attention to your sugar levels and staying in close touch with your obstetrician and internist. Or you may need insulin temporarily because you don't produce enough yourself to satisfy the huge demands of a pregnancy.

If you are normally controlled by diet and oral hypoglycemic agents, you must now switch to insulin until after the baby is born. This is because the oral agents will not only stimulate your pancreas but the baby's as well. Because it is not yet known whether the oral drugs cross over into breast milk, it is also recommended—if you are going to breastfeed—that you continue on insulin until weaning time if strict diet won't provide sufficient control.

Plan Ahead

Ideally, you should have your babies early in life. And you should plan ahead, decide when to conceive, get yourself in the best possible physical shape before you begin your pregnancy, because the first few weeks of life are the times when your baby's organs are formed. This means your diabetes is under good control, you are not overweight and you have resolved any important medical problems before you start off. Some doctors even recommend, as a prelude to pregnancy, that a diabetic woman check into the hospital for at least a few days for evaluation and glucose regulation. If you followed the earlier rules this should not be necessary. At least one study has demonstrated that the babies of women with the lowest hemoglobin A_1c (see pages 133–34), blood-sugar levels measured over a period of weeks, have the fewest abnormalities.

Once you are pregnant, don't waste a moment starting your prenatal care. Your insulin requirements will change radically and quickly. Good diabetic control—whether or not you take insulin—is particularly important during the first two months, the time when much of the baby's initial development occurs.

A team of medical experts will manage your pregnancy—an obstetrician, an internist, perhaps a dietician, laboratory technicians, later a pediatrician who specializes in perinatology. You will probably visit the obstetrician every week or two until about the thirtieth week, then more often after that. You may see the internist twice a month, and consult with the dietician now and then.

Conceiving Your Baby

If you are healthy, you can get pregnant just as easily as anyone else. Diabetes does not interfere with your fertility when you are well controlled. A diabetic husband, however, may be a source of conception difficulties (see Chapter 15).

If Your Husband Is Diabetic

Having a diabetic husband will not affect your pregnancy at all, whether or not you are diabetic yourself.

Choosing Your Obstetrician

Unfortunately, many good obstetricians do not have expert knowledge of the special problems of diabetic pregnancies. Nor do many hospitals have the facilities and laboratories you may need. Especially if you take insulin, it is essential that you check out the obstetricians and hospitals in your area. Much depends on the kind of medical care you will receive.

If you are already seeing a diabetologist (an internist whose specialty is diabetes), this doctor will know where to refer you. If you are not going to a diabetologist, we suggest you find one now, or at least an internist who has been recommended by your local Juvenile Diabetes Foundation or American Diabetes Association affiliate. You will need the services of this doctor along with those of the obstetrician. He/she must be available to you night and day—as this person should be even when you aren't pregnant.

The diabetic organizations will also recommend obstetricians, as well as the best hospital for you. Or you can call the department of obstetrics and gynecology at the nearest large hospital or medical school for the names of doctors with special expertise in diabetic pregnancies. Do not, unless you have no choice and no chance of moving, pick an obstetrician simply because your next-door neightbor likes him. You require a person who is an expert.

What Kind of Diabetic Are You?

Dr. Priscilla White of the Joslin Clinic has classified pregnant diabetic women into five groups, so that potential problems may be more easily predicted. The groups range from those with the mildest diabetic indications to those with the most serious complications. Obviously, women who fit in the early categories usually have the fewest difficulties during pregnancy because their diabetes has had less effect on their bodies' ability to go through the incredibly complicated process of creating a baby.

Class A: Gestational diabetics, women who have abnormal glucose tolerance during pregnancy only. For them, the condition is transient. They have no symptoms and diet is the only treatment they require.

Class B: Women whose diabetes began after age 20 and have had it less than 10 years. They have no evidence of kidney or eye disease.

Class C: Women who have been diabetic for 10 to 20 years, and were diagnosed between the ages of 10 to 19. Again, no evidence of serious complications.

Class D: Women who were diagnosed before age 10 and have had diabetes over 20 years. They have early retinopathy and/or some kidney damage, calcified blood vessels of the legs, or hypertension.

Class E on: Women with severe retinal, renal, heart, vascular or calcification disease.

Gestational Diabetes

Sometimes women who have never shown signs of diabetes will have abnormal glucose tolerance for the first time during a pregnancy, especially if they are 20 percent or more over their ideal weight. They are called gestational diabetics, and unless their diabetes preexisted and is only now being discovered, they can expect to lose the disease as soon as the baby is born. Usually they have no overt symptoms and simply require a good diet and sufficient exercise to keep their blood-sugar level normal so that their transient condition won't affect their babies or their deliveries. Occasionally, though, a gestational diabetic will develop very high blood sugar and may need insulin temporarily to bring it down to normal.

It's important to remember that this temporary abnormality **is a sign that diabetes may occur some time later in** life. And among women who deliver babies over 9 pounds at birth, about 25 percent develop the disease within five years, and 60 percent within 12 years.

What Is a Prediabetic?

A prediabetic is someone who is going to become diabetic, and many pregnant women fit into this group. Pregnancy puts a stress on the pancreas, and if your pancreas has inherited a tendency to diabetes, this may be the time when it will become apparent, the more likely the more pregnancies you have. If you are overweight, remember that every 20 percent of excess weight increases your chances even more.

Because pregnancy is such a common time for diabetes to show up, your obstetrician should perform a routine urinalysis in your third week (or just as early as possible) and again in your 28th week of pregnancy. Sugar in the urine, however, doesn't have to mean you are diabetic. During any pregnancy, the flow of blood to the kidneys increases and sugar absorption decreases, resulting in more spilled sugar than normal. So, if your urine tests are positive, you will now require a formal glucose tolerance test or an isolated sugar analysis after a meal to confirm the diagnosis.

What Is Different About a Diabetic Pregnancy?

Unless you have had diabetes for many years, have serious complications or are in poor diabetic control, you do not have a higher chance of miscarriage than any other woman. And you will probably carry your baby to term, or close to it. If your diabetes is more severe, your baby may be delivered early.

Because good control is the road to a happy and successful outcome, constant vigilance is essential. Along with scheduled visits to your doctors, you must test your urine or blood for sugar four times a day, adjusting your medication accordingly.

Though the insulin you take does not cross the placenta to the fetus, blood sugar does. This means that when your blood sugar goes up, so does the baby's. This stimulates the immature pancreas to produce too much insulin. Excessive insulin promotes the deposition of fat, and so, if you are a mild diabetic, your baby is likely to be quite large. This fact alone may mean you will need a cesarean delivery. With excellent control, you can keep your baby down to a more normal size.

Severe diabetics, however, sometimes have very small babies, because vascular complications involving the placenta may restrict the fetal blood supply and therefore the nourishment the fetus receives.

A frequent problem in diabetic pregnancy is hydramnios, an excessive amount of amniotic fluid, which can make you very uncomfortable and perhaps cause premature labor. At the first sign of hydramnios, you will probably be instructed to stay in bed to reduce the volume of fluid.

Other possible special problems include kidney and vascular complications as a result of damage caused by long-term diabetes; and toxemia, a condition that is becoming much less prevalent as knowledge of the value of good control increases. Because in pregnancy there is a greater tendency toward urinary infections, your urine should be checked regularly.

How Pregnancy Affects Your Diabetes

Because carrying a baby is a real stress on your pancreas, your need for insulin will skyrocket during your pregnancy, doubling or even tripling. But in the first trimester (up to 13 weeks), your need will probably *drop*, and you will have to keep adjusting your dose downward (with the help of your doctor) while watching out for hypoglycemic reactions. Reactions during these early weeks are very common and may occur without any warning, though medical consensus is that they won't hurt the baby. Don't make a move without your emergency sugar, be sure other people know how to handle possible reactions by giving you sugar or Glucagon injections if you can't take it by mouth, and make certain your doctor is always available for consultation.

The dip in insulin need is probably due to the large amount of glucose the developing fetus and placenta is using, along with the effect of other hormonal changes, and perhaps morning sickness. You may not be eating (or keeping down) as much food as you usually do. Try to eat foods that appeal to you, space them out in small amounts throughout the day. This phase will soon pass and many women don't experience it at all. If necessary, your doctor may prescribe an antinausea drug. Or, when you can't keep anything down, drink three ounces of *regular* ginger ale every three hours until the nausea passes. Do not drink diet ginger ale. You will need the sugar in the soda. Besides, it is best to avoid saccharine during pregnancy.

After the first two or three months, there is another big change. Now your insulin requirements start rising sharply and you must keep increasing your dose. Along with insulin shock, which remains a distinct possibility, you must be on the alert for the other extreme—acidosis. This, too, can come on very quickly now, and is a much more serious situation. If your tests are poor, if you have an infection, or if you are nauseated, very thirsty, breathless or have any of the other symptoms of high sugar, check with your doctor immediately. Untreated, acidosis can be harmful to your baby.

Toward the end, around your eighth month, your insulin needs will probably stop rising and will level off.

After the baby is born, they will make another dramatic drop. You may not require any insulin for a few days, or much less than your usual dose. Then gradually, within about six weeks, you will return to your prepregnancy dose.

Split Doses Are Best

Insulin-requiring pregnant diabetics do best with split doses, usually taking both quick-acting and Intermediate-acting insulin before breakfast and again before dinner. The Regular insulin takes care of breakfast and dinner; the Intermediate insulin takes care of lunch and the night, so that all bases are covered. In addition, you may need more shots if your sugar is high at any time during the day. You must respond to the information you get from your four daily blood-sugar tests.

If you never took insulin before your pregnancy, you probably won't need it after it's over. You may now return to your simple diet control or diet combined with oral agents. To return to oral agents, your doctor will probably ask you to take your prepregnancy dose and, if you are spilling sugar, to cover it with insulin before dinner and at bedtime. In a few days, you will know what your correct oral agent dose should be. If you are breast-feeding, do not go back to the pills until the baby is weaned.

What Is Good Control?

Though other numbers may be tolerated when you are not pregnant, good control at this time translates to a blood-sugar level of *no lower than* 70 mgs, and *no higher than* 100 fasting and 150 after a meal. This takes careful attention to your diet, and constant adjustments of your insulin if you require it. It's surprising how many women, after playing fast and loose with their diabetes for years, become model patients when they are carrying a baby. Their concern for the baby makes them change their life styles radically.

You must check your urine four times a day, before breakfast (second voiding), lunch, supper and bed, using a testing method that indicates high sugar levels clearly. During a pregnancy, the kidneys pass along more sugar into the urine and you will spill more than usual, even if your blood sugar isn't any higher than it normally is. So some sugar doesn't necessarily mean you are in trouble. Just to be safe, however, test for acetone and/or make a finger-stick blood test when your sugar reads high. Acidosis is always a distinct possibility during pregnancy, and it may happen very quickly, so you must be on the alert.

Home blood testing should become part of your everyday routine in any case as a way to double-check the urine readings, which may not give you a reliable indication of how you are doing.

When you take insulin, this is especially important. You may use Chemstrip bG or Dextrostix, testing strips that are read by eye, comparing the color on the strip to a color block on the bottle. Of, if you can spend the money, buy a reflectance meter, a blood-glucose measuring machine that gives you color-coded or digital readouts. See Chapter 8.

Blood tests are valuable even if your diabetes is diet-controlled. Always make a blood test if your urine shows more than 2 percent sugar.

Using the Insulin Pump

In the few instances when a pregnant woman's diabetes continues to soar out of control despite her best efforts, doctors sometimes recommend an insulin pump. This is a gadget worn around the waist. It infuses a few units of insulin per hour through a subcutaneous catheter and gives more before each meal, simulating the normal pancreatic output. Carefully attended, the pump can obviously provide excellent diabetic control.

Eating for Two

We haven't talked about total calories before, but now that you are pregnant, this becomes necessary. Most pregnant women require from 1,800 to 2,000 calories of food a day, but the amount that is right for you must be decided together with your doctor or a dietician. Be sure to eat everything on your meal plan and eat it *on time*. When you strive to maintain the excellent blood-sugar control that is so important now, insulin reactions (if you are insulin-dependent) are always a possibility, even after the first trimester.

When you are pregnant, you will need more protein than at other times. Include one glass of milk (skim or regular) at all three meals, as well as at your midafternoon and bedtime snacks. You may also increase your usual meat portion at dinner.

Space your food throughout the day so your blood sugar doesn't rise and fall sharply. Your developing baby needs a constant supply of nutrients.

Take a daily multivitamin tablet that includes folic acid.

"Will My Baby Be Healthy?"

If you're in good control and the baby is mature, he or she has just about as good a chance of entering the world in as good condition as any other infant. The baby will not be born diabetic. In fact, there is a likelihood of hypoglycemia—low blood sugar—for a few hours or days after birth. While still in the uterus, the fetus was exposed to your blood sugar and the tiny pancreas responded by producing large amounts of insulin. A short period of time is needed now to settle down to normal. The pediatrician will have blood tests made to see if the baby requires supplements of sugar given by bottle or intravenously to compensate for the excessive insulin still being turned out.

Other possible results of the baby's long exposure to high sugar include low blood calcium and high blood bilirubin (which causes jaundice), neither of which is cause for serious concern today. Your pediatrician will be alerted to these complications and can correct them. Jaundice rarely needs more than a few days' exposure to ultraviolet lights, and low calcium is treated with intravenous calcium infusions. Babies born to diabetic mothers are usually kept in the nursery's intensive-care unit for a few days for close observation and, if necessary, treatment. Premature babies, of course, may require much longer hospital stays and special care by a team of neonatal specialists, but most infants are ready to go home with their mothers.

"Will My Baby Be Diabetic?"

Your baby will not be born diabetic. But, with a diabetic parent, there is a one percent chance your child will develop diabetes before the age of twenty and a 12 percent chance of developing it in its lifetime. Those are not overwhelming odds when you consider that six percent of the general population has the very same risk. With two diabetic parents, however, the chances rise to about 50 percent sometime in a life span.

"Do Diabetic Complications Get Worse During a Pregnancy?"

They could, especially if you do not maintain excellent control. On the other hand, they may improve. One study of a group of pregnant women with retinopathy reported that a third of the women were found to have improved by the time of delivery, a third stayed the same, and a third got worse. If your eyes happen to get worse, they can be treated with laser therapy at the onset to forestall further problems. See Chapter 11. It has been found, moreover, that eyes that become worse during pregnancy usually go back to their former condition afterwards.

Though kidney problems may increase during a pregnancy, the tendency is to return to your prepregnant situation after your baby is born. In the meantime, kidney problems can make the pregnancy a little harder to manage.

Timing Your Baby's Arrival

Once it was true that many babies of diabetic mothers died in the last few weeks of pregnancy, and so it became customary to deliver the babies long before their due date. This led to problems. Because diabetic women sometimes have irregular periods, it wasn't easy to pinpoint the correct delivery time, and the babies were frequently brought into the world, usually by casarean, long before they were ready and suffered from all the problems associated with prematurity.

Today, however, sophisticated tests are available in large medical centers for measuring both fetal health and maturity. Every diabetic woman must be closely monitored, especially as she nears her due date, but Class A and Class B diabetics who do not have complications can often go all the way to term and deliver their babies in the usual fashion. More severe diabetics are delivered earlier, usually by the 38th week, but in most of these cases only after it is has been determined that their babies are mature enough for this world. In these cases, labor is induced or a cesarean section is performed.

Most obstetricians put their diabetic patients into the hospital for their last two or three weeks, so they can be closely watched. Usually, this is much the best place to be.

How does the doctor know how your unborn baby is getting along? One way is to make frequent checks of your estriol levels toward the end of the pregnancy. A hormone produced by the fetal adrenal glands is changed to estriol by the placenta and excreted via the urine. The level normally rises continually throughout pregnancy and is an indication that the baby is doing well. But if the estriol level does not rise, or if it drops, then the doctor may decide the uterus no longer provides the best home for the baby and that it would be better off delivered early.

Estriol tests ideally should be made twice a week from the 30th week on in more severe cases, from the 35th week on in uncomplicated cases; then every day after you are hospitalized, just to be certain the baby is still safe.

The oxytocin challenge test is another way to find out if your unborn baby is healthy. In this procedure, the technician will fasten two belts around your abdomen, one which records the baby's heartbeat, the other your uterine contractions. You are given a small dose of oxytocin, which makes the uterus contract slightly, while the fetal heartbeat is watched to see if it remains normal.

Testing for Maturity

Not many babies of diabetic mothers are delivered too early today, because now there are standard tests available at all large hospitals or in laboratories to determine whether they are mature enough to be born. The major problem of premature babies is respiratory distress syndrome (RDS), which means that the tiny lungs are not yet prepared to breathe air efficiently.

To predict lung maturity, amniotic fluid is tested for the presence of a substance called surfactant, which lines the air spaces of the lungs and helps in breathing. If enough surfactant is being produced, the baby's lungs are considered to be developed enough for delivery.

Sonography is another way to test for maturity. Pictures produced by sound waves, started very early in pregnancy, can monitor the rate of the baby's growth so that maturity can be estimated.

Sometimes the obstetrician will decide it is best to deliver your baby even though the lungs are not fully mature. In this case you may be given corticosteroids, which usually stimulate the production of enough surfactant within only 24 hours to ensure a safe delivery.

"Can I Breast-feed My Baby?"

Being a diabetic mother doesn't affect your ability to breast-feed except that getting started may be a little more difficult if you are separated from your baby for very long after the birth. But even if you can't start immediately, it is quite possible to express your milk manually or with a pump so you will continue to produce it until you need it.

The baby will not be affected by the insulin you take, and won't have insulin reactions. You will probably require less insulin while you are breast-feeding because the baby is consuming some of your glucose supply in the milk, so be alert to your own possible reactions and make adjustments in your dosage if your sugar tends to fall very low.

Because breast-feeding can cause rapid drops in glucose levels, be sure to have a carbohydrate snack before each nursing session.

You must also adjust your diet, adding about 600 to 900 calories a day to compensate for the amount you are expending. Extra milk is an excellent way to get those calories.

Because lactation can cause false readings with some of the urine-testing methods, use Tes-Tape while you are breast-feeding. This reacts only to glucose and not to the lactose, a form of sugar that is now in your urine.

Remember that you must not take oral agents while you are breast-feeding. If diet isn't doing the job of controlling your blood sugar, you must take insulin temporarily.

FIFTEEN

Sex
and the
Diabetic

Does being diabetic affect your sex life? If you are a woman, the answer seems to be "no." But if you are a man, there is a chance the answer could be "yes." It is estimated that about a quarter of middle-aged diabetic men who have had the disease for many years, who suffer from neuropathy and probably have not maintained very good control, become impotent. Though sexual difficulties can obviously be psychological (and often the anxiety about the possibility of future problems can cause them), in most cases an organic disfunction quite specific to diabetes is the reason for an increased incidence of impotence, at an earlier age than the rest of the population.

What occurs is not loss of libido or desire for sexual gratification, but the ability to have an erection. This ability may gradually diminish and eventually vanish completely. Usually the cause is neuropathy damage to the nerves responsible for stimulating the arteries in the penis to dilate and produce an erection. This is almost always associated with other neuropathies, often in the legs and feet and, most likely, the bladder.

Occasionally the reason is an obstruction or clot in one of the blood vessels supplying the penis, and sometimes poorly controlled diabetes causes temporary impotence as a result of a general weakened condition.

Possibility of Impotence

Though some studies have been made, it is still uncertain just how many diabetic men eventually develop sexual problems by middle age. Uncertain, too, is whether impotence is related to the severity of the diabetes. Probably it is affected by the quality of blood-sugar control over the years, and the number of years since the diagnosis was made.

This does not mean that impotence is in the cards for every male diabetic—there are men who have had diabetes for fifty years and have no problem—nor that all is lost and nothing can be done about it.

First, it must be determined whether your impotence, which never happens suddenly but comes about gradually when it is caused by diabetes, is psychological or physiological. Your internist will suggest an examination by a urologist and perhaps a neurologist, and if there is no obvious physical reason for the problem, may suggest an NPT (nocturnal penal tumescence) assessment. This is usually performed in the sleep-disorder department of a large medical center, and monitors the nocturnal erections that normally occur at regular intervals while a man sleeps. If you have normal nocturnal erections, then you are not suffering from nerve or vascular damage and psychological counseling will probably be recommended. If your neuropathy is the culprit, you will not have erections in your sleep or any other time.

Obviously, if your impotence is the result of poor diabetic control, then good control is your answer.

If the cause is vascular obstruction, sometimes surgery can make a dramatic difference.

Dealing with the Problem

When your problem is neuropathy, there are several things you can do. Check with your doctor about a drug called Mytelase, used in treating myasthenia gravis. This has proven to be effective for some men by increasing the function of the nerve endings. This drug must be administered very carefully, however, because it sometimes produces a very uncomfortable side effect—violent cramps that require immediate doses of atropine to counteract them. Other therapies, too, will surely evolve before long.

Though there is no way to repair damaged nerve endings, you may want to look into the possibility of a penile implant or an inflatable device, both of which are designed to allow sexual intercourse complete with ejaculation and orgasm. When you have an implant, flexible silicone rods are placed in the penis, making it rigid enough for intercourse. A problem is that the penis remains rigid.

The more complex "inflatable erectile prosthesis" allows actual simulation of a natural erection by the implantation of a device that inflates and deflates the penis on demand.

Another possible helpful aid is a vacuum constriction device that gives the penis rigidity. This is a non-invasive technique and may be worth a try before resorting to implants.

Obviously, a diabetic man's wife should have a voice in the decision about an implant, and may want to help the situation by doing an exercise that builds up the vaginal muscles to make them tighter and more able to hold a somewhat thinner penis. This is called the Kegel exercise: alternate tightening and releasing of the vaginal-rectal muscles for a total of about 10 minutes a day. This can make sex more satisfying for both partners.

Effects on Fertility

Diabetes doesn't affect a man's ability to produce sperm, so, assuming he is not impotent, there's usually no reason he cannot father children. Sometimes, though, diabetic neuropathy will cause a condition known as "retrograde ejaculation." Because the nerve supply to the penis is impaired, the sphincters won't open and the semen, including the sperm, drops back into the bladder. This doesn't interfere with intercourse or orgasm, but obviously precludes fertility.

Sex and the Diabetic Woman

Though we know that diabetes does not affect a woman's ability to have sexual intercourse, and it is thought that it also does not affect her ability to have orgasm (though one study reports a lower incidence of orgasm among diabetic women), she may have other related problems as a result of her lowered glucose tolerance.

One is an increased tendency toward vaginal and urinary infections. The high sugar environment when you are in less-than-ideal control promotes the growth of bacteria and yeast. Add to that the sometimes diminished ability of the white cells to rally around and fight infections. If you notice any signs of vaginal or urinary infection, get yourself to your doctor immediately. There are drugs which can alleviate them, usually in short order. Along with the drugs, however, you must get your diabetes back in good control and keep it there.

Vaginal dryness is another problem that often accompanies poorly controlled diabetes. This will improve along with better control and, in the meantime, can be counteracted by the use of a lubricant made for this purpose. By the way, do not use petroleum jelly which will inhibit your own secretions.

What Kind of Contraception?

For the diabetic, probably the best countraceptive methods are the mechanical kinds—the diaphragm or the condom. These present no problems, as long as you remember to use them every time.

Next best, according to a team of researchers who made a recent study, may be progestogen-only oral contraceptives. Taken every evening near dinnertime, these pills seem to be highly effective and without side effects except for a much higher incidence of irregular menstrual periods.

The usual oral contraceptive—the "pill"—is not a good idea for several reasons. Most important, some studies have shown that the hormones in the pill can lower your glucose tolerance. Because you may not handle your blood sugar as well, your insulin supply may not be as effective. The pill can also make your already sticky blood platelets become even stickier, promoting the possibility of clots and cardiovascular disease. And it can increase your chances of getting vaginal infections by changing the ecology of the vagina to a state more inviting to various bacterial and fungal invaders.

Many physicians think that the IUD, the intrauterine device, is associated with increased vaginal infections. Diabetics need no more ways of acquiring infections. In addition, according to researchers, there is a high failure (pregnancy) rate among diabetic IUD users, probably because of an unusual metabolic interaction of the device with the endometrium, the uterine lining.

For those couples who do not want children or have completed their families, sterilization is an option.

Changes in Insulin Needs

For many women, insulin requirements change the week before their menstrual period, so you should check your urine and respond accordingly. Your pattern of needing more or less insulin at that time will usually remain consistent.

If You Use an Insulin Pump

Obviously, it may be uncomfortable to have sexual intercourse while wearing a bulky pump. If you can't find a satisfactory position, it won't be harmful to detach it for a while, just as you do when you take a bath.

SIXTEEN

Traveling: Diabetics on the Move

IF you are just a beginner at this business of being a diabetic, you probably are afraid to travel. You feel much safer at home. You are not interested in surprises, not when you're away from your own kitchen, your own medicine cabinet and especially your own doctor.

But, once you have learned the rules, whether it involves only diet or includes insulin or pills, and you have had sufficient practice coping with the variations of a diabetic life, then there is no reason you cannot travel anywhere in this world like anyone else. But you must remember, just because you're breathing the pure mountain air of the Alps or savoring the sights of Hong Kong, you have not left your diabetes behind you. It travels with you. So the same rules apply wherever you are.

There are a few precautions that a person with diabetes, especially one who is insulin-dependent, should take. Let's run through them briefly. If you are not yet an experienced traveler, you may want to slip this book into your luggage for handy reference.

A Before-You-Go List of Suggestions

• Don't travel (and that means anywhere, including the next town) without some visible medical identification affixed to your person. Wear a bracelet or necklace stating "I am a diabetic," and carry two cards (one in your pocket, another in your wallet) that say the same and also list your medication and allergies, along with your name, address and phone number. If possible, carry a card in the language of the country you are visiting.

• Before leaving town, go to your doctor and have a checkup to be sure you are in good shape for your venture. Don't go anywhere when your condition isn't stable. Check out with your dentist too, so that you don't find yourself in Afghanistan with a toothache and an askew blood-sugar level. Go to your podiatrist, because you will undoubtedly be doing a lot of walking and you should be sure there is no foot trouble brewing. Take along an extra pair of eyeglasses, or a least a copy of your prescription. Many a person, not necessarily diabetic, has toured Europe out of focus after losing his/her only pair of glasses the first week out.

Be Prepared for Problems

• Ask your doctor to prescribe an antidiarrheal medication to take along, just in case you'll need it. Lomotil and paregoric are effective for treating the symptoms. Antibiotics, such as Bactrim or Septra taken twice a day, will treat the disease itself.
paregoric are effective.

If you are going to a country where you are fairly sure to run into intestinal problems, there are medications to take as preventives *before* trouble strikes. According to a Johns Hopkins University School of Medicine study, a single dose of Doxycycline, an oral antibiotic, protects most travelers from diarrhea. For some people, though, side effects can include gastrointestinal upset and hypersensitivity to sunlight. Or pack some Pepto-Bismol. Studies have shown that two ounces four times a day can usually keep you out of trouble if you start taking it at th'e first twinge of an upset. Of course, a suitcase full of Pepto-Bismol may be hard to carry along on your trip! You can buy it almost everywhere you might go. A side effect for some people is constipation.

Also take along an antiemetic to prevent or treat nausea. If you are susceptible to motion sickness, take the preventive four hours *before* you board the boat, walk into the airplane or step into the car. Be sure to take along some antiemetic medication in suppository form in case you can't keep anything down. Remember, too, that medicine like Compazine, effective against nausea, can be injected with your insulin syringe.

A new treatment for motion sickness requires only that you place a special medicated sticker behind your ear.

• Take along a note from your physician stating that you are a diabetic and require insulin. That's so the customs inspectors, coming upon a supply of syringes, won't suspect they have uncovered a drug addict who must be turned over to the gendarmes. The statement will also help you buy more syringes if you need them.

• Carry a large enough supply of oral agents or insulin and syringes *to last the entire trip*. Always include a bottle of Regular fast-acting insulin, even if you normally take only longer-acting insulin or none at all. In an emergency, this will be essential.

• Take plenty of blood-sugar testing equipment. Most people prefer the strip tests for traveling.

Don't Be Caught Short

• Insulin need not be refrigerated. It will survive nicely for a few months in any environment that's comfortable for you. Never allow it to become excessively hot (don't let it sit in the sun or in a closed car) and don't let it freeze. This means it must *not* be packed in your luggage if you fly, because temperatures are often below freezing in the baggage compartments. Oral hypoglycemic agents are not harmed by freezing, however.

• Carry your insulin and some syringes, or your oral drugs, *with you* in your hand luggage to cover those possible occasions when you go one way and your luggage goes another. This is important. It won't be harmed by the airport X-ray machines. Disposable insulin syringes may be used more than once. Seven syringes can be adequate for two weeks. After use, simply recap the needle.

• If you take insulin, carrying your own is especially important. In many countries, only U-40 is available. But don't panic if you run short—it's really quite simple to convert your usual dose to U-40. See Chapter 7.

• Your brand of insulin will probably be available in other countries, but it may help to know that, in Europe, Regular or fast-acting insulin is often called Actrapid. Semilente may be known as Semitard or Sultardum. Rapitard or Lentard or Monotard would correspond to our NPH or Lente insulins. Ultratard would be equivalent to Ultralente. The initials "MC" after the name signifies "monocomponent" insulin, which is simply a purer and less allergenic form of insulin that has only recently become standard in the United States. In most cases, the dose would be the same or slightly less than your accustomed dose of nonmonocomponent insulin.

You may want to write to the manufacturer of the insulin you use (well before your departure date) to ask about its availability in the countries you will be visiting. You can avoid all problems by carrying plenty of your own with you.

• A good trick to remember is the 1-cc tuberculin syringes can be substituted for U-100 syringes where each line equals one unit of insulin.

• If you take oral agents and need to buy more, you will find counterparts available in foreign countries. Here are some of the equivalents:

Orinase (Tolbutamide)		*Tolinase (Tolazamide)*	
Artosin	Europe	Norglycin	Germany
Diabin	Japan	Orabetta	Chile
Dolitol	France	Tolanase	England
Mellitus D	Japan		Canada
Mobenol	Canada	Tolisan	Denmark
Oralin	Philippines		Iceland
Orsinon	Israel		
Rastinon	Europe,		
	Canada		
Yosulant	Mexico		

Diabinese (Chloropropamide)		*Dylemor (Acetohexamide)*	
Catanil	Italy	Dimelin	Japan
Chlorodiabet	Spain	Dimelor	England
Chloronase	Germany	Ordimel	Norway,
Diabetoral	Germany		Netherlands,
Mellinese	Denmark		Sweden and
			Chile

In some places, only an agent called Daonil (Glyburide) available. This is the equivalent of Diabeta or Micronase and in the same family as Glucotrol. You may use it as a substitute, taking just one tablet a day.

Speaking Their Language

• If you are going somewhere where a language other than your own is spoken, memorize in the appropriate lan-

guage (and write in clear lettering on a card) the following phrases: "I am a diabetic." "Sugar or orange juice,
please." "Please get me a doctor."
Here they are in four languages:

I am a diabetic,
French: *Je suis diabétique.*
Spanish: *Yo soy diabético.*
German: *Ich bin zuckerkrank.*
Italian: *Io sono diabètico.*

Please get me a doctor.
French: *Allez chercher un médecin, si'il vous plaît.*
Spanish: *Haga me el favor de llamar al médico.*
German: *Rufen Sie bitte einen Arzt.*
Italian: *Per favore chiami un dottore.*

Sugar or orange juice, please.
French: *Sucre ou jus d'orange, s'il vous plaît.*
Spanish: *Azúcar o un vaso de jugo de naranja, por favor.*
German: *Zucker oder Orangensaft, bitte.*
Italian: *Zucchero o succo di arància, per favore.*

• Another precaution before you leave home:
Though you certainly hope it won't happen in the middle
of a great vacation, there's always the possibility of getting
sick and needing a doctor, whether you are diabetic or not.
It is always best to be prepared. Write to the American Diabetes Association (1 Park Avenue, New York, N.Y.
10016) for a list of affiliate or chapter offices of the Association wherever you plan to travel within the United States.
If you need a doctor in Cleveland, for example, a call to
the Clevland Diabetes Association will get you a list of
local doctors experienced in diabetic care.
From the same national ADA office or from the Interna-

tional Diabetes Federation (10 Queen Anne Street, London W1M OBD, England), you can get a list of diabetes associations in foreign countires. (Telephone: London 01–6367–3644.)

When you arrive at your destination, remember that the U.S. embassy or consulate will supply the names of English-speaking physicians upon request. So will the major hotels.

Travel Tips On Your Way

Now you have finally had all the proper checkups, your diabetes is under excellent control, you have gathered your supplies together, tucked away all those lists and statements. You are ready to get your show on the road. *And* you do not want to hear any more advice. However, we have a few more tips, all designed to make it easier for the traveler who happens to have diabetes.

• Most people who take medication for diabetes are concerned about their schedules for insulin or pills when they cross time zones. When you travel by car or ship, no problem. The time changes are so gradual they will not affect your time table. Simply take your medication at your usual hour according to the time it is wherever you are.

If you take oral agents, do the same, even if you fly long distances, crossing many time zones. Take the pills according to your new time.

But when you fly long distances and you take insulin, it gets a little trickier. Here's how to handle it.

Keep your watch set at your point-of-departure time, so you will know how many hours have passed since your last injection. Eat your meals and snacks on your normal schedule, according to the time on your watch. If you have forewarned the airline and reminded the steward when you board the plane that you must have your meals on time because you are a diabetic, he will then try to serve you at your accustomed mealtimes. (And, of course, you will not have set forth without your usual emergency snack supplies.) If meals at different times from those of the other passengers seem to be too difficult to arrange, board the plane with your own box of food.

On arrival, if *more* than 24 hours have passed since your last injection, take a few *extra* units of Regular insulin and/or Intermediate insulin. However, if *less* than 24 hours have passed since your last injection, take *fewer* units of Intermediate-acting insulin because some of the dose you took the previous day is still in your bloodstream. If you are skipping a meal, you must adjust for less food.

After taking your insulin, set your watch to the time of the place you now find yourself in, and start taking your injections accordingly.

Going from West to East

Suppose, for example, going West to East, from the U.S. to Europe you have taken your insulin shot at 7A.M. on the day of departure. You leave New York at 6 P.M., arrive in Europe at 2A.M. our time. But it is 7 A. M. European time. It's OK to go to sleep, skipping breakfast on land, and get up before noon when it is 24 hours from the time of your last shot. You are going to have only lunch and supper on this day. Your insulin, therefore, should be based on *two* meals and reduced by about 20 percent. Now set your watch on European time. The next morning, take your usual dose.

Remember to adjust your insulin to your physical activity. If you will be much more active than you normally are at home, you must compensate by taking a few less units of insulin or eating more food (see Chapter 5).

Going from East to West

Now, what about coming home, from East to West? Or traveling West from the United States to the Orient? Let's use this example: You take your insulin and depart from Europe at 8 A.M. You arrive in New York seven hours later —3 P.M. European time, 10 A.M. New York time.

You have had breakfast before getting on the plane, and you have eaten lunch during the flight. Your next meal is supper at 6 P.M. European time, noon in New York. Eat your supper then. Eat your bedtime snack at 11 P.M. European time, 7 P.M. in New York.

Go to bed early. When you wake up, you are five hours late for your next shot. Take a little more of your Regular insulin and the usual dose of long-acting insulin. If you are not on Regular insulin, take your usual dose of long-acting insulin and eat less starch for breakfast.

• Never make a move without your cache of emergency carbohydrates. You must have this *with* you at all times, just on the chance—however remote it may be in your case —that you will have a hypoglycemic reaction. Sugar cubes, candies, cookies, crackers. Don't carry sugarfree candies which won't help you a bit if you have low blood sugar.

• If you are traveling by car, and especially if you are the driver, take the equivalent of 10 grams of carbohydrate every hour: two graham crackers, an orange, 15 grapes, whatever.

Now You Are There

Once you have arrived at your destination, simply start living in your accustomed way, adjusting your medication to your blood-sugar level and your physical activity just as you would at home.

A few things to keep in mind:

• You may be much more active on vacation than you are in everyday life. If you are going to do strenuous sightseeing, play tennis, ski, swim, anything that burns up considerable sugar, you will require more food or less insulin. Oral agents are not so critical and do not have to be adjusted. On the other hand, if you overindulge, you cannot expect an extra pill to correct it, as you would if you were on insulin and took an extra dose when your sugar was high.

Suppose you plan to play a few tough sets of singles, make a cross-country ski trek or even do some heavy sightseeing on foot.

Check your urine. If it is negative, eat extra carbohydrate and protein before setting off. If it is positive, have some carbohydrate after about an hour of exercise. Or reduce your insulin as an added precaution against reactions. Sometimes you will need snacks every half hour or so of heavy exercise. See Chapter 5

• Never ski, swim, bike, hike or climb alone, but always rely on the buddy system. If you should have a reaction, your buddy will cope with it. Unless you started off with high sugar, the exertion may drop your blood sugar very quickly to subnormal levels.

Keep Your Shoes On!

• Remember if you have foot problems not to go barefoot, even on the beach. One sharp shell can get you into long-term trouble. Don't get sunburned. A burn is a burn, and the stress it causes can throw off your control.

Use foot powder, wash your feet and change your socks frequently. Keep an eye on your feet, giving them a daily inspection. Unaccustomed walking can produce blisters and rubs, especially if you are wearing new shoes. Do not let any foot injuries get even the slightest bit out of control. Rest your feet, take the pressure off, wear sneakers, sandals or slippers if necessary, and if trouble seems to be brewing, see a doctor *immediately*, not two weeks after you have returned home.

• Watch what you eat. Nobody wants a gastrointestinal upset, but diabetics can have their whole vacation ruined by the after-effects and the difficulty of getting their blood sugar back under control. In tropical countries, don't eat raw vegetables, soft cheese, ice cream, rare meats, cream sauces, fruits you can't peel. Use bottled or boiled water even for brushing your teeth. Don't drink fresh milk or water, and avoid ice cubes. One man bought an unpeeled melon in India, thinking he could eat it safely. But his host served it to him cut up and floating in ice water. He had his melon, plus a good case of amebiasis and diarrhea.

• If you get up late and miss breakfast, take about 20 percent less insulin because you'll be having only two meals that day. Don't try to make up for the lost meal by eating more now, because that will present you with too much carbohydrate to handle at one time.

Dining Fashionably Late

• In some countries—Spain, for example—the dinner hour is late. If you plan to have your meal at the fashionable hour of, say, 10 P.M., then you must prepare in advance. There are two ways to handle this situation. Either take less insulin in the morning and give yourself a second shot before going to bed, or consume the major portion of your carbohydrate allowance (the equivalent of two slices of bread) at 6 P.M., then eat everything else—your main course, vegetables, dessert—at dinner. Of course, you will then skip the carbohydrates at the table—rice, corn, potatoes, bread, etc. This also applies to weddings and other parties here at home.

• Be sure your traveling companions know how to cope with both hypoglycemia (low sugar) and hyperglycemia (high sugar). Your companions should know that you need quick sugar if you are having an insulin reaction—granulated sugar, honey, a soft drink (not a diet drink), candy, orange juice, etc., followed shortly thereafter by some protein. Or you may be given "instant glucose" which comes in a toothpastelike tube and can be forced through the lips. If this isn't quickly effective, a subcutaneous shot of glucagon and a doctor may be necessary. Have all the supplies always handy. See Chapter 9.

If you are suffering from *high* sugar and acetone (and this must be checked out with a urine or blood test), then you need insulin and perhaps the service of a doctor.

• Adjust the eating customs of the places you visit to your own needs. This means making sure you get the right proportions of carbohydrate, protein and fat, no matter where you are. A continental breakfast, for example—a roll and coffee—isn't going to be enough for you unless that is what you normally consume at home. Order additional food. Many foods, notably a lot of Chinese and Japanese dishes, contain sugar and must be avoided. Sukiyaki, for example, is made with sugar or sweet wine.

Remember your carbohydrate exchanges: 1 cup of rice is the equivalent of 2 slices of bread, or 30 grams of carbohydrate. So is one regular-size pita, even if it is flat as a pancake. Some tropical fruits, such as mangos, are very high in sugar. Check them out before eating them freely.

• Wines and liquors needn't be avoided, if you drink them in moderation, as you do at home. See pages 69–70.

• If you happen to get sick away from home, treat yourself just as you would in your natural habitat. See Chapter 12. Test your urine four times a day for sugar and acetone. *Always take your insulin.* If your tests are negative *and* you can't eat, take half your usual dose of insulin. If your sugar is high, whether you can eat or not, take your regular amount. Always take your normal dosage of oral agents.

If you are spilling sugar and are vomiting, take your full insulin dose. Then take an antiemetic by suppository. Eat or drink some carbohydrate every hour—perhaps 3 ounces of orange juice mixed with water, or 3 ounces of ginger ale (*not* sugar free), or ice cream, toast, broth, cereal, etc. Don't tough it out—if you need a doctor, get one.

Traveling Is Fun, Remember?

With all these precautions and pieces of advice, perhaps you think it might be simpler to stay home. But make all your preparations, keep the advice in the back of your mind just in *case* you need it, and go forth, not to worry, but to enjoy yourself. You take your diabetes with you, but other people take their problems with them, too, and may not be as carefree as they seem.

Enjoy.

SEVENTEEN

Down the Road In Diabetic Research

So much diabetic research is currently going on in this country and in other parts of the world that the life of a person with this all-too-common disease is certain to change in amazing ways in only the next few years. Startling breakthroughs have brought real promise of marvelous new treatments, even hints of prevention and cure. Here is a brief rundown of some of the most exciting developments:

Synthetic Human Insulin

Using new gene-splicing techniques, scientists have successfully induced bacteria to produce insulin that is biologically identical to the insulin made by the human body. After clinical tests, the new synthetic insulin is now mass-produced in bacterial "factories," and promises to provide a plentiful source of insulin, which now requires 16,000 pounds of animal pancreas glands to come up with 2.2

pounds of the hormone, enough for 1,650 average diabetics for a year. The new gene-spliced insulin as expected results in fewer allergic reactions to injection.

Automatic Insulin-Delivery Systems

The "open loop" insulin pump now used by relatively few diabetics has wrought near-miracles for some who never before could achieve good blood-sugar control. The pump delivers, via a catheter usually attached subcutaneously, tiny amounts of insulin every few minutes in a predetermined pattern that may be adjusted to anticipated requirements. Before meals it releases a larger amount, approximating as closely as possible the insulin output of a normal pancreas in response to food. The pump, which is worn attached to a belt, is still relatively new and presents problems that remain to be solved.

In development now is a "closed-loop feedback" system that may become a real substitute for one's own pancreas. This consists of a sensor that continuously measures blood-glucose levels and a pump that releases the appropriate amounts of insulin in response. Many problems persist with this device; present models are the size of a television set and so complex that they require highly trained operators and specialized medical resources.

Glucose Alarm Watch

Another invention in the works is a wristwatch that senses lowered body temperature and perspiration and signals when blood sugar falls too low, alerting the wearer to impending insulin reactions. This would be especially helpful to diabetics who tend to have reactions while they are sleeping. One defect: You may get false alarms if you sweat during the night.

Transplants

The transplantation of pancreatic islet cells, which is biologically feasible in experimental animals, has not yet been successful for human beings. But when it does become workable, this disease can actually be cured. The current major difficulty is the problem of immune rejection—the cells are eventually treated as foreign invaders and rejected by the body.

Implanted Insulin Depots

A molecular depot of insulin to be implanted in the area of a blood vessel, sensitive to glucose levels and able to release insulin, is another possible breakthrough of the near future. This capsule would control blood sugar in much the same way as a normal person's pancreas does. Other techniques envision the implantation of live beta cells capable of secreting insulin, and a compound of a sugar chemical and insulin that would release the hormone when blood sugar rises.

Vaccines

Vaccines could make juvenile-onset (IDDM) diabetes a disease of the past. The discovery that several viruses can cause diabetes in laboratory animals and in man, and evidence that a virus can trigger the later nonfunctioning of the beta cells, has spurred research into the possibility of vaccines that could immunize children against the viruses. The vaccines, given to all children or to those who are "genetically marked" as predisposed to diabetes, are currently the best hope for diabetes prevention.

Synthesized Somatostatin

The hormone somatostatin inhibits the secretion of other hormones, two of which—glucagon and the growth hormone—work against the lowering of blood sugar. Researchers are trying to synthesize somatostatin that can be added to the insulin injection to make the insulin work more effectively.

New Genetic Markers

The search goes on for new markers that indicate who will become diabetics. It has already been found that a raised level of activated T lymphocytes confirms an active immune reaction in newly diagnosed insulin-dependent diabetics. If the presence of these cells proves to be a true marker for diabetes, it may be possible to reverse the progression toward the disease with drugs now under investigation.

For additional information and help, contact your local affiliate of the American Diabetes Association (national headquarters: 2 Park Avenue, New York, N.Y. 10016) or the Juvenile Diabetes Foundation (national headquarters: 23 East 26 Street, New York, N.Y. 10010).

Index

About the Authors

STANLEY MIRSKY, M.D., F.A.C.P., Diplomate of Internal Medicine, is associate clinical professor of metabolic diseases at the Mount Sinai School of Medicine in New York, and is on the staffs of Mount Sinai, Lenox Hill and Doctors hospitals. He is President of the Professional Section of the American Diabetes Association, New York Diabetes affiliate, and a member of the board of directors of the New York Diabetes Association. Dr. Mirsky is also on the board of directors of the Joslin Diabetes Center, Inc., in Boston, Massachusetts, and a counselor with the Lahey Clinic in Boston. He is the former chairman of the Clinical Society of the New York Diabetes affiliate of the American Diabetes Association; he has written extensively on the subject of diabetes. Dr. Mirsky was an editorial associate of *Diabetes Forecast*, a magazine published by the American Diabetes Association. He lives in New York City.

JOAN RATTNER HEILMAN is a freelance writer of books and magazine articles. A former magazine editor, she has co-authored many books in the health field, including *The Complete University Medical Diet*, *The Nachtigall Report on Menopause*, *Having a Cesarean Baby*, *The Complete Book of Midwifery*, and *The Story of Weight Watchers*. She lives in Mamaroneck, New York.